LETTERS FOR OUR CHILDREN

Letters for Our Children

Fifty Americans Share Lessons in Living

Erica Goode, *Editor*
with Jeannye Thornton

Foreword by
James Fallows

Photographs by Jim Lo Scalzo

A *U.S. NEWS & WORLD REPORT* BOOK

RANDOM HOUSE NEW YORK

Library of Congress Cataloging-in-Publication Data

Letters for our children / [edited by] Erica Goode :
with a foreword by James Fallows.
p.   cm.
ISBN 0-679-45011-4 (alk. paper)
1. Conduct of life—Case studies.   2. Children—United States—
Conduct of life.   3. Role models—United States—Correspondence.
4. Role models—United States—Biography.   5. Success—United
States.   I. Goode, Erica.
BJ1581.2.L474   1996
170'.44—dc20   95-43150

Random House website address: http://www.randomhouse.com/

Printed in the United States of America on acid-free paper

24689753

Book design by Carole Lowenstein

Foreword

James Fallows

It's hard to envision the drama of other people's lives. Most of us move through the years acutely aware that our own lives have a dramatic and moral structure. We have disappointments and successes. We measure our progress against our own standards and against the lives of our rivals and friends. We come to crossroads, and we make our choices. Whatever choices we make, we are never free of regrets. We plan endlessly for the future, as if we had an endless number of tomorrows to deal with. We think about the past and try to form our yesterdays into a story with a meaningful plot.

Meanwhile, we may be strongly tempted to view the rest of humanity as props—movie-set extras—for the drama that centers on us. We see them walking on the street, driving in their cars, taking their children to fast-food restaurants—and we may be lured into assuming that the big decisions have already been made for these other lives. By the way these other people dress, the kinds of jobs they hold, their age and accent and race, we may feel that we know all about them. It would be rare to say it quite this directly, but most of us act as if the choices still ahead for other people, and the meaning of their pasts, cannot be quite as complex, richly dramatic, or carefully balanced as the choices in our own lives.

Works of great literature succeed and survive precisely because they break through this barrier. Charles Dickens, Jane Austen, and any of a thousand other writers are considered great because they convince readers that the inner struggles of invented characters can be as engrossing as the readers' own lives. Only a handful of the writers who have produced the letters in this volume are publicly known figures. But collectively the letters qualify as literature. They show us people from a wide variety of backgrounds trying to make sense of the choices in their lives, and the letters make those choices gripping, even if we have never heard of the people involved.

The idea behind this collection was even more powerful than its originators could have known. In most circumstances, people are tempted to suppress or shy away from a fully honest reckoning of their life experiences. We all have failures, which we prefer not to dwell on. We may overstate or misremember the nature of our successes. But the exercise of presenting lessons to our children draws most people up to an unusual level of honesty. If these lessons are to be of any value, they must be completely honest; and the effort to provide useful guidance for the next generation has pushed most of these writers to a degree of candor about themselves that would be hard to sustain in day-to-day life. The achievements the writers are proud of—having kept a marriage together despite strain, having stood by friends and relatives when times were tough, having given customers and business associates honest value through many decades of dealings—seem earned achievements, not boasts.

The far more impressive theme—in fact, the dominant theme of this book—is not achievement but the art of coping with heartbreak, failure, and sheer, unfair bad luck. A gun stored in a car's glove compartment goes off accidentally, and a young man spends the rest of his life in a wheelchair. A teenage girl, without a husband, agonizes about whether to keep or give up for adoption the baby she is about to bear, only to see the baby die of a heart defect a few days after its birth. A woman whose specialty is trying to prevent divorces sees her own relatives shattered by the effects of a divorce. To a surprising degree, these letters are an elaboration on the theme that "Skipper" Duncan, a cattle rancher in West Texas, calls, in his letter to his stepson, "Don't Flunk Failure." In school, Duncan says in his letter, "failure" merely means a bad grade. Sooner or later in adult life, however, it will mean something more:

> We're talking shipwreck here. A hollow feeling will settle in the pit of your stomach and there will be a load on your shoulders that is more real than figurative. A sense of impending doom will stalk you day and night.

"So how will you handle failure when it comes?" Duncan asks. Many of the letters in this book are attempts to wrestle with that question, no matter the different ways various people may phrase it. It could be sobering to think that when parents are asked to pass on to their children their most important life lessons, they so often dwell on adversity. But that would be depressing only if we had the childish faith that things will never go wrong. The real message of many of these letters concerns the human art of resiliency. "Never get discouraged," Ralph Levy writes to his grandson after sixty-two years with the Fuller Brush Company. "Life has its ups and downs, but if you will set goals and then work hard, even through adversity, you will do well."

In isolation, comments like these may seem platitudes. In context, they show fifty people struggling to derive a pattern and meaning in their lives. These fifty letters from Americans stand as representatives of two hundred fifty million other struggles, by these writers' countrymen, to draw lessons and derive meaning.

Contents

Introduction

When the first of the letters gathered in this book arrived on my desk at *U.S. News & World Report*, I opened the envelope unsure of what I would find inside. From the beginning, the project was a gamble. We planted seeds, but had no idea what would grow from them. A collection of letters written to children about the things adults care most deeply about, we believed, could offer an intimate, compelling window on American values—indeed, the idea for the book grew out of a much smaller group of such letters that appeared in *U.S. News* in August 1994, part of a package on "America's Values Crisis." Yet so much would depend on the letter writers themselves: Would they reach beyond platitudes and homilies? Would they take their task seriously? What would they have to say?

In choosing contributors last year, we tried to put together a cross section of American lives. We wanted real people in this book, not just celebrities or politicians or experts of one sort or another. We pored through newspaper clippings, searched through library stacks, talked to colleagues and friends, contacted service organizations, churches, and professional groups. By the end, we felt we had been pretty successful at recruiting participants from a wide variety of occupations, religious denominations, economic classes, political orientations, cultural backgrounds, and life circumstances.

More difficult was conveying to letter writers, once they were in place, exactly what we hoped for. In phone conversations and in a cover letter, we described how we envisioned the book, and offered the following guidelines: Write a letter to a child you care about, to your son or your daughter, your grandchild or your niece, to a student or to the child of a friend. Write about the things that are most important to you, the lessons you have learned in your own life that you would like to pass on. Tell stories. Offer tools for survival in a complicated world. Avoid preaching. Say the things you might not be able to say in person, or over the phone. We were aware of the dangers of trying to write about everything at once, and suggested that contributors choose a focus for their letters, a topic arising out of their own lives.

In other words, we laid what groundwork we could, and waited to see what would happen. Yet had we spent six more months in the planning stages, I don't think we could have predicted the process we were setting in motion, or anticipated how gratifying and involving would be the results.

Over the next months, contributors called us often. At the start, we knew little more about most of them than we had gleaned from our brief interactions in soliciting letters. But as the summer unfolded, we began to learn more. We heard about their lives, we talked to them about their hopes and worries for their children and grandchildren, we coaxed and encouraged them, answered their questions, helped them meet deadlines and sort out scheduling problems. Inevitably, some participants dropped out; others took their places. *U.S. News* photographer Jim Lo Scalzo, who put thousands of miles on rental cars traveling around the country to complete the pictures for the book, got to know the final group of writers even better than we did, meeting their families, sharing meals with them, bringing back images of faces and houses and landscapes to merge with names and biographies, with the voices we heard over the phone.

In late June, the first letter arrived, and by midsummer almost every other day brought another thick envelope or fax. Some submissions were handwritten, some typed on ancient manuals, some computer-polished and primped, like young boys dressed up for Sunday choir. A few letters logged in at under five hundred words; others ran to twelve single-spaced, typed pages. Each arrival brought a new salutation: "To My Daughter Angela," "Dear Billy and Tricia," "Dear Children and Grandchildren of All Ages." Each ended with its own avowal of affection: "Yours, Popi Max," "With love, Dad," "I will love each of you always and forever, Your Mom." Some came with notes attached:

"Enclosed is the letter I had agreed to write. Not as easy as one would think," wrote one contributor. Offered another: "I'm afraid what I've submitted is probably not what you're looking for. In that case, a gentle rejection will be okay."

One morning in August, as I waited in an endless line to have my car inspected, I began leafing through the stack of letters on my lap—my first chance to read them as a group, one after another. I moved from a ranch in Texas to an Indiana doorstep where a Fuller Brush salesman waited. I listened to a woman with AIDS talk to her niece about regret, to a doctor tell his son about doing the right thing, to a Vietnam veteran fulfill a promise to a dead friend. And I realized that something quite extraordinary had happened: The voices we had brought together were now a chorus; the individuals who five months before had been strangers now formed a community.

Some readers of these letters will be startled by the unity of vision that emerges from such vastly different lives, the concerns and imperatives voiced by a conservative Christian family in Iowa not so divergent from the dedication to integrity and self-discipline expressed by a lesbian military nurse in Seattle, though neither might condone the particulars of the other's moral code. Others who read these pages will be struck by the differences in the letters, by the idiosyncratic lens through which each contributor sees the world. Few of these authors are published writers, but in many cases, the force of an individual letter derives from the fact that only this person, at this time, in this place, could have written it.

But at the heart of this book lie its stories, family stories stored up and cherished, sometimes handed down from generation to generation. Stories are a way of making meaning, and every writer represented here is a meaning-maker in a profound sense, extracting power and cohesion not only from life's largest dramas—losing a parent or a child, facing a disability, dealing with an illness—but also from its smallest events: kissing your children's socks when they come out of the dryer or trying to field the baseball in a Little League game and booting it instead.

We came up with the idea for this project, gave it a name, helped it reach completion. But in the end, this book belongs to the parents and grandparents, uncles, aunts, teachers, and neighbors who accepted our invitation and reached deep inside themselves to answer it. We were often moved by their candor, by their struggles, by their fears for their children and their loving attempts to point the way. We hope you will be, too.

ERICA GOODE
U.S. News & World Report
Washington, D.C.

Awakenings

"Life owes us nothing. Because of the goodness
of others, we are here."
MAX HELLER

Max and Trude Heller with their children and grandchildren

Extreme heat melts snow, Max Heller says, but it also hardens steel. Which may help explain how Heller and his wife, Trude, refugees from Hitler's death grip on their native Austria, managed to retain their faith in human beings. "One act of simple human kindness wipes out a lot of bad experiences," says Heller. "I believe that people can be good. You have to tell this to yourself or else you become so pessimistic about life."

A chance meeting, a man who reached out to help a stranger, a series of small miracles—these were the events that allowed Heller to find a new life in South Carolina. A fan of American movies and culture even as a child in Vienna, he quickly adapted to his new home, working in a shirt factory, branching out to start his own business, eventually becoming mayor of Greenville in 1971. Now semiretired, Heller enjoys the luxury of relaxed mornings with Trude in the brick-and-redwood house they built in a quiet Greenville neighborhood forty years ago. Their only complaint: The dining room is now too small to seat their children and grandchildren on their frequent visits home.

Dear Children and Grandchildren of All Ages:

I was going to address this letter to just one of you, but how could I possibly choose? So this is to all of you. The other evening we (Mopi Trude had much to do with this letter) watched an old movie. The movie was in black and white, and what some people might call "corny," that is, it was about family, love, jealousy, responsibility, etc., and in the end, everything came out happily. Today, some might call it a fairy tale. So be it, but really, why shouldn't the good survive and triumph?

The movie made me think of my maternal grandparents, my grandfather Samuel and his wife, Miriam. They lived in Lubacow, a small town in Poland. Their home was very modest and very clean. They were a religious family, observing all dietary laws and the Ten Commandments. Grandfather had a very unusual profession: He made a livelihood by hand-engraving wooden boards with different patterns—flowers, dots, trees—and he printed these designs on fabric that people brought to him. My grandparents' greatest pleasure came from family and their complete faith in God. Though their lives were in constant danger from anti-Jewish attacks by peasants and soldiers, they had absolutely no fear. "God will protect us," they said. My mother, Leah, grew up in that environment, and at age twelve was sent away to Kraków to escape pogroms and the attacks of drunken soldiers out to rape Jewish girls and beat up any helpless Jew. It is hard to describe to you how much hatred and violence our family suffered. You might think that in such a climate my grandparents and my mother would have lost faith in people and in God. Well, they did not. Faith was all they had. They certainly were not wealthy people. They were honest, hardworking, minding their own business, and they always hoped for a better tomorrow.

I remember every visit with my grandparents, and I loved every moment, as I listened to their experiences, their wisdom. I never heard them complain, and they never considered themselves poor. Strangely enough, what is still in my mind is the cleanliness of their home. Their body odor was one of water and soap—my grandmother used no perfume or even lipstick. My grandfather's beard was slightly stained from tobacco, and I could smell it. But most of all, I remember that theirs was a happy home.

My mother was married in Kraków to my father, Israel, and moved to Vienna while he was in the army during the First World War. This is where both my sister Paula and I were born. As we got older, my mother would tell us of her escape from Poland, and her happy life with her parents, and she would also sing beautiful, sad songs. God, how I loved being near her, listening to her songs and learning about life.

One might think that life was beautiful in Vienna. The truth is that while life in our home was good, Vienna itself was full of paradoxes. Austrians loved good music and good food, and were well-educated, religious folk. Yet they had the ugly sickness of anti-Semitism. Even during my youth—going to school, for instance—I would have to fight, because other youngsters jumped on me, accusing me of having killed their Christ. I think you will be happy to know that I fought back, and many times I came home with a bloody nose. My mother was so horrified that I would tell her, "Oh, but you should see the others!"

So with all the problems, life went on. I went to a private high school, finished early and at age fourteen, went to work as an apprentice in an

Austrian company which was starting "dime stores" like those in America. Within two years, I became a manager there, and I thought I had a good career with the company and a good life ahead.

Then, in 1937, during my vacation, two things happened that had a tremendous impact on my future. My parents rented a house in the country not far from Vienna. There, I met a beautiful, tall, blonde, blue-eyed girl and fell in love with her instantly. Trude was fourteen and I was seventeen, and I told her that I was going to marry her one day (she blushed).

During the same week, I decided, for no real reason, to return to Vienna for a day, coming back to the country with my father on Friday for the weekend. When I got off the train in Vienna, I met a friend of mine and we decided to go dancing. We went to a beautiful outdoor restaurant and sat all evening listening to music and watching the people. Late in the evening, I noticed a table with five attractive American girls and a chaperone. (The fact that I had fallen in love with Trude did not prevent me from looking at other girls!)

There was one girl in particular at the table I was drawn to, so I asked her to dance with me. After a conference with the chaperone and her other friends, she agreed, and we danced until the place closed. I asked her: "Could I take you for a walk tomorrow?" I bought a German/English dictionary and we walked for two hours, making conversation through the dictionary.

When I took her back to her hotel, I told her I would learn to speak English, and I asked if she would give me her name and address. She wrote it on a piece of paper: Mary Mills, on Mills Avenue in Greenville, South Carolina. I put the paper in my wallet. Then I went back to the summer resort and told Trude about my meeting, and about dancing with the American. She was not too impressed.

That week in 1937 decided the rest of my life. I met both Trude, the love of my life, and Mary Mills, who saved my life later on. On March 11, 1938, Hitler came into Austria and the Austrians were jubilant. People received him and his troops with open arms, happy because, for one thing, they were given carte blanche to do as they pleased. Stores owned by Jews were broken into and plundered; synagogues were burned; people were beaten up. All that happened within the first few days.

That Friday night, as always, my mother lit candles and said the prayers, and we had a Sabbath meal as we did every week, but we also talked about the future. I said that I thought we should leave Europe. "There is only one place to go," I said, "and that is America." "Who do you know in America?" my parents asked. I reminded them that I had kept the address of the American girl I had met the year before, and I said I was going to write to her. I tell you now that nobody believed that she would remember me. But I wrote anyhow, and begged her to help me.

In the meantime, conditions in Austria continued to get worse. The place I worked was taken over by a Nazi who formerly had worked for the company. One day he walked in with four of my co-workers, all wearing Nazi uniforms and swastika armbands, and confiscated the business. The irony is that he made out a receipt. Every Jewish person, with the exception of four of us, was fired.

We continued to live in fear: Every knock on the door, every footstep in back of me made my heart stop. My parents lost their business: Their customers simply stopped payments. Our bank account was confiscated. My mother sold off jewelry and silverware so we could have enough money for food. I was beaten on the street by a "friend" from school. I complained to the police, but they just laughed.

Yet our spirits were not extinguished. My father believed: "God will help." My mother believed: "God helps those who help themselves." So every day, we waited for mail from America, and one day, weeks later, a letter from Mary Mills arrived. I will never be able to tell you what it felt like to open that letter. It meant my life or my death. And there was Mary Mills saying to me, "I have not forgotten you! I have gone to see a man in Greenville by the name of Shepard Saltzman who told me that he would help you!" Can anybody imagine what it felt like to have that news?

Soon after, I heard from Shep Saltzman. He said, "How can I not help you? I am a Jew and Mary Mills, a Christian, wants to help." What a lesson in life that is. It tells us that this is what it is all about: people helping people. On July 20, 1938, my sister Paula and I left Vienna. I had $8.00 in my pocket and a ticket for the boat trip. We were sad to leave our parents (they came several months later, through another miracle), but at eighteen, I was not afraid to face a strange country. I was ready to begin a new life.

After I arrived in America, I went straight to Greenville, where I found open arms and a job in Saltzman's shirt factory ($10.00 a week and grateful for it!). Most of all, I had freedom, freedom, freedom! The intangible. The precious. Despite the horrors of Hitler and the inhumane treatment by our former friends and neighbors, I believed that there is goodness in the world and that one good deed can overcome the evil of others. Mary Mills and Shepard Saltzman were my angels. Mary never realized what a wonderful thing she had done; Saltzman never doubted he should help. They saved my life and the lives of my family. Now they are resting in peace.

Your grandmother Trude did not have as easy a time as I. It was much later when she and her parents escaped from Vienna, but that is another story.

I have always felt that it is okay to believe in miracles. Never, never give up. Have hope. Trude and her mother finally got a visa to come to America. Her father was to embark two days later, but another tragedy occurred: Hitler overtook Belgium that day, and Trude's father was put on a cattle car with hundreds of other refugees and shipped to a concentration camp in the south of France. Ultimately, he escaped to Marseille and found his way to the United States.

I said I was not going to preach or lecture, and I am trying not to. But there are some things I must say: Sometimes things happen in life that we can neither control nor explain, and each of us reacts to these things differently. Some people never get over their unhappy experience; their wounds never heal, and continue to bleed. Trude's and my scars healed. We think of the good people who helped and cared. We think of the wonderful life we have together, the freedom we found here, the blessing of having you, three wonderful children, and ten grandchildren. Life owes us nothing. Because of the goodness of others, we are here.

We want to convey to you that there is more good than bad in this world. We don't dwell on the unhappy days. Yes, we mourn the ninety members of our families killed in concentration camps, but we also celebrate the living. We have learned what is important in life and we are grateful every day.

So, this is a long letter. When we are gone, the events in our life will be history. But we leave behind the most precious gift: having given life to you. Treasure it. We have so much faith in you, in your goodness, in your values. We are optimistic about the future. Thanks for being our children and grandchildren. Share your love.

Yours,
Popi Max (and Mopi Trude)

The noise when the gun went off was deafening. The pain was immediate and intense, as if his whole body were burning up. He thought he was dying. That accident, twenty years ago, changed Terry Winkler's life, put him in a wheelchair, tested his faith, his will to live, his strength of character. There were times when his determination weakened, when he sank into self-pity and depression. But he wanted to be a doctor, and neither his injuries nor the obstacles placed in his way by society would deter him.

Winkler—co-founder, with Dr. Spencer Lewis, of the American Society of Handicapped Physicians—now has a thriving practice in Springfield, Missouri, a short drive from the stone cottage on three hundred acres where he lives with his wife, Janice, a daughter, Shana Cain, and his grandson, Justin, three. Justin and his grandfather have a lot to say to each other. On any given afternoon, they can be found riding down to the pond to feed the ducks, Justin sitting happily aboard Winkler's motorized wheelchair.

Dear Justin,

I know you wonder why your "Papa" is in a wheelchair when your friends' grandparents aren't. You've never asked me about it, but I have seen you looking bewildered, even though you excitedly yell, "It's Papa!" when you see me.

Justin, there are some things I have always wanted to talk to the people closest to me about, but I've never had the courage. I guess it took more trust than I had at that point.

Through the years, there has been a lot of pain associated with my wheelchair and my disability. But there have also been many good things, and I have learned some things that I do not think many people ever have the chance to learn. You are the best little buddy I have, and I love you and want to share some of these things with you.

Long before you were born, I walked and ran and played just as you do. Then, at 2:45 A.M. on March 6, 1971, my life changed totally. I was

"The circumstances you find yourself in
are not nearly as important as your attitude
toward those circumstances."
TERRY WINKLER, M.D.

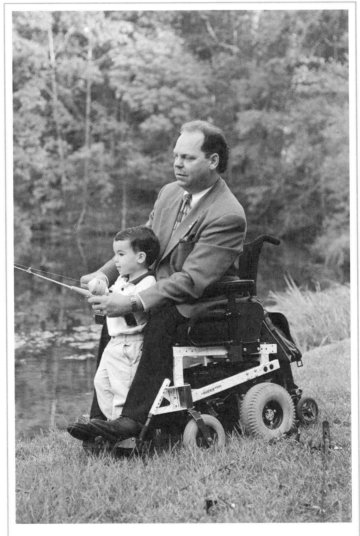

Terry Winkler and grandson Justin

eighteen years old, working in the oil fields in southern Louisiana. That night, I was riding with a friend in his '67 Chevy Impala. I was looking for matches—I was a smoker then—and I reached into the glove box, where my friend kept a loaded .22 Luger. I pulled the gun out, searched around for the matches, then tossed it back into the glove box. It went off, and the bullet crushed two vertebrae in my spine and severed my spinal cord, paralyzing me from the waist down.

The pain was excruciating. Even the hair on my head seemed to burn like fire. As I lay on the table in the hospital emergency room, people were rushing around, starting the IV, drawing blood, and preparing me for surgery. Maybe it was from the loss of blood or from medications, but I had a strange experience as I lay there, confident that I was dying.

I struggled to stay awake, but it seemed impossible, and as I drifted off, my spirit left my body. I have read of "out of body" experiences people have had, and they talk of a bright light that greeted them. My experience was nothing at all like that. I seemed to be sitting in a far and distant place, on a pedestal or stool, and it was total darkness, darkness so heavy you couldn't even see a few inches in front of your face. I looked down, and the only thing that I could see was myself lying on the table. And that person, who was me, could look up and see me sitting in some far and distant darkness. I could see all the doctors and nurses running around, and I could hear everything they were saying. And the person or spirit that was out of my body was saying, "This is it. You are gone. You are dying."

The next thing I remember, I was in my hospital room and the surgery was over. I was unable to open my eyes, and all I could hear was people mumbling, and all I could think was, "What are these people doing in my casket?"

There is one thing that I know for sure as a result of that experience: It was not a hallucination. I have studied science in some of the best universities in the world. I have graduated from college cum laude. I have won scholarships to Harvard University, and I have studied medicine now for years. But this experience taught me beyond a shadow of a doubt that there is another life after this, and there is a God—don't ever let anyone teach you or tell you different.

The emotional impact of my injuries was immediate and devastating. At first, it seemed to be a bad dream, but reality persevered and my feelings turned into anger and resentment. Why me? Why couldn't it be fixed? The uncertainty of my future was incredibly frustrating. All that I thought that I knew about myself had been washed away.

As the reality of disability sank in, I became severely depressed. I would stay in bed for weeks at a time, completely dependent on my family for care. There were years of illnesses, repeated infections, and more surgeries—I lost count at thirty. This continued throughout my entire college years and during the time I was at Harvard. I spent more time each day caring for my wounds than most students spent studying.

Not being able to walk was the easy part. I had more trouble with the other parts of my life. For one thing, I had a very bad attitude regarding my disability. I had doubts and fears about my self-identity and self-worth, and I was consumed with a tremendous uncertainty about my future.

It took me a long time to realize that my attitude was the biggest problem with getting on with my life. The first thing I found out was that "Why me?" leads to a procession of unanswerable questions and serves no useful purpose whatsoever. So I changed "Why me?" to "Why not live your life to the fullest?"

The next thing I found out was that I was OK. Even though I couldn't walk, I was still a good person, and there was still value and merit to my life. And gradually, my attitude toward myself began to change to a more positive one.

I also realized that I had a bad attitude toward my wheelchair. I viewed it as a prison. Every morning when I woke up, I knew that if I moved at all, it would be from the confines of a cold, steel chair. I saw it as a shackle preventing me from accomplishing my will, as something that directed my life. But slowly, I realized that that wasn't the case at all—that, in fact, I directed the chair. If I wanted it to go to the left or to the right, it would. If I wanted it to go to college or to Harvard or to medical school, it would. And it did. The only change was my attitude. I began to see the wheelchair as a tool that I used to accomplish my goals in life, nothing more.

The thing is, holding on to a positive attitude is not easy. I was not prepared for the way that my friends and society in general treated me. They felt that I was someone who was sick. When I would go into restaurants, the waitresses would raise their voices and simplify their language, as if I couldn't understand what they were saying to me. If an able-bodied person was with me, people would not even talk to me, ignoring me and asking the able-bodied person questions about me.

When I knew that I wanted to be a doctor, I went to the vocational rehabilitation counselors and told them about my goal. They said it was unrealistic, that I would never be accepted to medical school, and they wouldn't help me go through college to be a doctor. In the end, I had to major in something else and double up on my course work to get my premed courses completed. Then, after making excellent grades and sometimes the highest grades in the science classes that I took, the director of the premed admissions committee also told me that he thought I wouldn't get into medical school, and that therefore the committee could not give me their recommendation. I slowly began to realize that I was being judged not by my grades or my abilities, but by my disability. These people meant well, but they had no idea what I could achieve, and they certainly didn't know what was in my heart.

Justin, as you go through life, when you see people who are different from you, don't assume that they are not smart, or that they are not good people. You have to recognize that they are just like your Papa. They are different, but they are still OK. They still have value, and they should be given the basic right to make decisions regarding their lives.

When I got to medical school, there were more people who felt I should not be there. There was one professor whose job was to teach physical diagnosis and internal medicine. During the first week of class, he sent a message for me to come to his office. When I got there, I immediately recognized the look on his face. I had seen it hundreds of times before: the look of a person who had already made a judgment about me based on my disability. He wouldn't look me in the eye. Finally he said, "It is my opinion that I can't teach physical diagnosis to a person in a wheelchair, but I've been told by the dean to give you a satisfactory grade if you can pass the written test."

I was infuriated that he judged me that way. Here I was among physicians, the people who I thought really understood, and their attitude was no different. I looked straight back at him, and I said, "You don't have to teach me physical diagnosis. All you have to do is stay out of my way and I'll teach myself." And I did.

There were other things that happened that I want to tell you about. Once, I pulled into a 7-Eleven, and there were two little boys there. They were a lot like you: One was about seven; the other, perhaps five. They stared at me as I pulled my chair out of the car and went past them into the store. Every aisle I went down, I would look up and they would be watching from the other end. Then, when I was at the cash register paying, I saw them outside, their little faces pressed against the glass. As I went out, the littlest one said, "What's the matter with you, did you break your leg?" And the other one poked him in the side and said, "No, stupid, can't you see he's got cancer?" Their faces and expressions have become one of my fondest memories over the years, but in a subtle way they mirrored how society in general felt about me.

I could go on about the things that worked to produce a bad attitude. But what is most important are the things that generated a positive feeling, and that have turned out to be the most important things that ever happened in my life. I believe that there is a certain beauty in the lives of disabled people. A disabled person is someone who deals with all the issues in life that everyone else deals with, and then many more, as well. And there is some part of our spirits or our souls that doesn't seem ever to be willing to give in to a disability.

The first thing that helped me occurred when an old friend, Bobby Dye, came by the hospital and visited when I was very sick. I had been in a wheelchair for two or three years. Bobby had become a preacher, and he asked me if I knew the Lord. I told him that I didn't. He said, "Terry, there is a scripture in the Bible that I think is the saddest scripture in the world. It is in the book of Matthew. People are standing before the Lord, and it is Judgment Day and they are asking to be forgiven, and saying 'We did a lot of good things in our life.' And the answer to them is 'Part from me, you workers of iniquity. I never knew you.' "

When he was saying all these things to me, I wanted more than anything in the world for him just to stop talking and leave. The things he was saying made me angry and very uncomfortable. But I could never get them out of my mind. And several years later, I realized that he was right.

At the time, I was unable to sleep at night. I was totally reliant on my mom and my family because I was so depressed, I wouldn't care for myself. One night, in the middle of the night, I prayed and said, "Lord, I know that there has to be more to life than what I have." I asked for forgiveness, and I asked for God to help me. There was no lightning or thunder, but slowly things began to change. I began to read the Bible, and there was one verse in particular that stayed with me through the years. Every time I was in a bad situation, where people were not accepting me because of my disability, or when I was sick, or when it seemed like I would never get into medical school, I would think about that verse: "Just like a tree planted by the waters, I shall not be moved." That one verse took me from being a high school dropout to Harvard, to medical school, to a private practice, and to the beautiful life that your Granny and I have now with you as our grandson. That faith and trust in God brought a whole new light to my life and restored a positive attitude for me.

The last positive thing I want to tell you about is Dr. Lewis. Dr. Lewis was perhaps the greatest friend that I've ever had. When I was in college, he came and spoke to our class about diabetes mellitus and its effects. Dr. Lewis knew this well, because he was a diabetic and he was totally blind. But he was also a physician, and practiced medicine in Gambling, Louisiana, and he had attended Harvard Medical School. He welcomed me with open arms, as another disabled person who wanted to be a doctor. I would go and work in his office every day after class. Together, we founded an organization to help other disabled people become physicians, called the American Society of Handicapped Physicians.

Dr. Lewis told me about the Harvard Health Professions Program and I applied. But between the time I applied and the time I received the letter of acceptance, Dr. Lewis died very unexpectedly. He was the most positive, intelligent, upbeat man that I'd ever met. He was the first person who actually believed that I could be a doctor.

I was overwhelmed with grief. I couldn't believe the tragedy. Dr. Lewis was only thirty-six when he died, and he left three children behind. I thought I would never live through that. His body was brought back to his little clinic where he had practiced medicine in Gambling, and I sat beside his casket in shock and disbelief. But it was there that I learned another lesson about attitude.

This lesson came from Dr. Lewis's lifelong friend, Fred. As I sat there, I felt such a tremendous loss, and I told Fred that I just couldn't understand and couldn't accept what had happened. But Fred told me, "Terry, Spencer Lewis was a wonderful man. But as tragic as his death is, the greater tragedy would be if you didn't accept and recognize the gift that he has given you." I knew immediately that what Fred said was true. Each person that you know in your life, Justin, has a gift to give you. Dr. Lewis's gift to me was a gift of a positive attitude, and he made me realize for the first time that I could be a doctor and that nothing could or would stop me from achieving that goal.

I thought I'd never get over Dr. Lewis's death, and I never have completely. But I've learned that there is a balance in life, such that every great loss is offset by an equally great gain. For example, I lost the ability to walk and I have to use a chair. But I've gained the ability to be a physician and to be a grandfather for you.

Justin, there are many things that will hurt you as you grow. There are a lot of things that will happen in your life that you won't understand. In fact, you are already experiencing changes that hurt. Your Mom and Dad are separated and you can only see your Dad in Louisiana, and it means you can't be with them both, together. It's normal for you to wish it wasn't that way, and I know that at times it's confusing for you.

I hope that problems you encounter in your life won't be of the same magnitude as the ones I've faced. But there will be problems: lost ball games, girlfriends who break up with you, cars that won't run, and many other things that will go wrong throughout your life.

But Justin, what is most important is how you view those things. The circumstances you find yourself in are not nearly as important as your attitude toward those circumstances. It doesn't really matter that your Papa can't walk, or that he is in a wheelchair. What matters most of all is how Papa feels in his heart about being in a wheelchair, and I feel that I'm a beautiful person, and that life has been good to me. I hope you will feel the same way about your life.

Love,
Papa

"You have to take your eyes off what you don't have
and place them on what you do have."
GWENDOLYN ROSE BRADFORD WILLIAMS

Gwendolyn Williams with Chloe Page Price

They are graduating today, and the luncheon in the Zodiac Room at the downtown Dallas Neiman Marcus is in full swing: Little girls in white dresses march in, their backs straight, their tummies tucked in, their voices polite and clear as they recite what they have learned in six weeks of classes at Pink & Pearls Charm and Etiquette. Gwendolyn Williams is the founder and guiding light behind the program, a place, she says, where children from diverse backgrounds learn to walk, sit, and stand with grace, to show proper manners, to respect their elders, but most of all, to believe in themselves and their abilities.

This last lesson does not always come easily, as Williams knows from experience: Disastrously burned in a childhood accident, she spent years rebuilding her confidence, slowly reclaiming her self-esteem with the help of a caring teacher. Now she can say: "I exude such confidence you would never know I had such scars." And most important, she can give something back, passing on what she has learned to children like Chloe Page Price, six, who graduated from Pink & Pearls in 1995.

Dear Chloe Page Price:

If I were to glance in a mirror when I was your age, guess what? The reflection would be a little girl who looked very much like you, with smooth, dark skin the color of Valentine's Day chocolate, big expressive eyes, and wavy ponytails, always tied with white satin ribbon. How happy and full of energy you are.

I am particularly proud of you at class introduction time. You walk before the class, chin up, shoulders back, tummy in, standing with perfect posture with your hands cupped together like a princess. Emily Post would have been proud. Your mother, Joycelyn, has placed much care in your uniform. Your blouse is always starched a crisp bright white, and your black pleated skirt lies perfectly in place.

As you move toward the center of the class, all eyes on you, your words ring out, "Good morning. My name is Chloe Price, I am six years old, I was born September 4, 1988, and I attend Maryview Academy. I like to paint and color. My favorite color is orange, and I want to be an artist."

Some of the boys, restless before, and squirming in their seats, and the girls who were twirling their hair and looking out the window, now give you their full attention. Chloe, as you speak, I see my six-year-old face reflected in the mirror of your tiny face. I remember when I had that confidence. I also remember the day I lost it.

One cold winter morning, I was standing near a heater to warm myself in the bedroom of my childhood home on Wise Street in Alexandria, Louisiana. Suddenly, the nightgown I wore, a white frilly gown with nylon ruffles, ignited and burst into flames. Red, blue, and orange flames chased me and, as I ran, caught me. My younger sisters watched, helpless and horrified, as I screamed with pain. My mother, outside hanging laundry, heard me and ran inside, grabbing me and putting out the flames with her bare hands.

After much surgery, and a year filled with skin grafts, therapy, and much pain, I was a different little girl. The person who had once said proudly to her kindergarten class, "Good morning, my name is Gwendolyn Rose Bradford," now sat at the back of the room. My body was scarred with third-degree burns. The left arm I once raised high when I knew the answer to a question was now slightly paralyzed. The doctors said that, with therapy, it might function properly again, and I believed that someday it would, being optimistic as a child. But my parents later told me that I would never be able to raise my left arm all the way: It was burned too severely.

I have shared with you the day I lost my self-esteem. Now let me share with you the day I found it again.

My parents, Major and Eloise Bradford, were positive people. We did not have a lot of money, but our home was filled with love, self-respect, and appreciation for things with which you have been blessed.

After being burned, I often wore long-sleeved dresses to hide my scars. One day, I was in physical education class, and we had to dress in shorts and a short-sleeved blouse. I was mortified, and I ran away, hiding in the gymnasium locker room where students showered. One of my classmates told the instructor, Mrs. Dorothy Moseley, that I ran away. She came to find me, and asked, "Why are you hiding?" "Because they're going to laugh at me," I said. Mrs. Moseley replied: "Some of them will, but some of them won't. You have to take your eyes off what you don't have and place them on what you do have."

I had heard this all my life from my parents. But on that day, it finally came home. I walked out, and walked across the gymnasium floor. Some of the students stared and pointed. But not all. A few smiled and said, "You wanna play with me?" And I smiled back.

I learned valuable lessons that day. The day I had assumed would be the worst in my life was the day I found my self-esteem. From that day to this, I keep my eyes on how I have been blessed.

Chloe, there is an old saying, "When life tosses you a lemon, make lemonade." My grandmother, Rosie Lee Berry, says, "Sometimes in life you don't even get a lemon, so you have to make sweet water." Know that, as you grow up, there will be obstacles that will make you want to sit in the back row of life. But also remember that it is everyone's right to sit in the front row. To do this, you have to first believe in yourself. Keep your eyes on what you have been blessed with. And, for those hard times when you don't get a lemon, remember to make sweet water.

> I love you, Chloe,
> Gwendolyn Rose Bradford Williams

"We all struggle with doing the right thing.
We do it simply, courageously, and daily."
TOM BRODERICK, D.O.

Tom Broderick and son Currie

*As an eight-year-old, the son of a factory worker in the Catholic world
of Bristol, Connecticut, Tom Broderick stood in church one day, waiting
his turn to step into the confessional. Suddenly, the woman ahead of him
fainted, pulling the heavy purple curtain down with her as she fell. The
boy was terrified. "Jesus, what did she do?" he wondered, and vowed,
"I'll never do anything that bad, or if I do, I won't tell God about it!"*

*Thirty-six years later, Broderick sometimes wishes "right" and
"wrong" were still so clear-cut. Instead, life turns out to be a murky
business. Now a doctor in Vermont, he makes split-second decisions in
the emergency room, raises his nine-year-old son, Currie, muddles
through with family, patients, and friends, and tries the best he can. But
even in medicine, trying one's best doesn't always mean things will come
out right: "The difficult thing is accepting that we don't always make the
proper call, that we are very human, and very fallible."*

Dear Currie,

As I stumble further into middle age, awkwardly navigating the maze
of my daily life, I am constantly reminded of the complexity of choices.
Life is intricate, colored by countless shades of gray, endless ambigui-
ties. Perhaps more than ever, we live in dangerously convoluted, head-
spinning times. Yet despite all this, there does exist an absolute, an
immutable truth.

Not long ago, I saw a movie entitled *Do the Right Thing*. The content
of the film quickly left me, but the title, and its significance, did not. To
me, "do the right thing" is the Golden Rule, applicable everywhere I
look. Indeed, I think of this phrase a couple of times each day. It hovers
in my mind when I consider the events of my own life. It grows even
larger and more important when I see you and your brother and sister
moving through your own young twists and turns.

When I was growing up, my idea of the "right" thing began with my
parents and the Catholic church. As European immigrants, my parents'
sturdy faith buoyed them through war and depression. Yet the Church
also tortured them with a sense of guilt, absolutism, and righteousness

that pitted them against much of the rest of the world. To my kid's mind, this worldview seemed reasonable. But at the same time, it did not seem to apply to my daily life at all: False gods and adultery were not burning issues to an American kid growing up in the 1960s. Nor did the Church's teachings help me sort out the thousand little decisions I was faced with each day, when I had to choose how to act, what to say, or what to think.

As I have grown older I have learned, on my own, about doing the right thing. It has not been easy. I have found that the options are: Do the right thing, something less than the right thing, the wrong thing, or, worst of all, nothing. I want it to be different for you, easier. Perhaps by telling you a few of my stories you will understand.

Your mother and I had only been married a few years when I started medical school. We moved a thousand miles from Connecticut to Michigan so I could attend the postgraduate equivalent of a four-year boot camp. Mom left a job and a group of close friends that she truly loved. Unfortunately, once there, we could not replicate those wonderful days in Connecticut. Mom ended up with an uninspiring job, one friend, and an absentee husband.

Our tolerance for one another's needs was stretched to a worn thread. In many ways, it seemed the best thing might be to go our own way, to get a divorce. So many people seemed to be making that choice that it was tempting. But your mother and I hung in there. In those years, we learned tolerance, finding that a little could be just enough. We learned to remind ourselves that in a few years (it seemed an entire lifetime), things would probably get better. Sixteen years later I know that we did the right thing.

When I was a neophyte doctor I cared for a forty-three-year-old woman schoolteacher, Eleanor, who suffered what we call "a hypertensive crisis." Her blood pressure was wildly elevated, and if it was not lowered rapidly, she was likely to suffer a heart attack or a stroke. She might even die. The medicines used for this lifesaving task are potent ones and not without risk, drugs that I would not use blithely. I was young, bold, and self-assured, trained to believe in and to expect the best outcome. Confidently, I told Eleanor about the risks and the benefits of the medicine, about what I proposed to do.

I remember as I slowly emptied the syringe of medicine into her intravenous line that I had Eleanor's complete trust. In my most reassuring tone, I told her that things would quickly improve. And then I remember the look in her eyes, the most helpless look I had ever seen, as she murmured "I'm dying." Her blood pressure plummeted to 0/0. The medication overwhelmed her. I recall sweating maniacally, wishing that I hadn't given her the drug, shouting frantic orders to the nurse. I remember praying. It wasn't the wrong medicine, the wrong dosage, or the wrong diagnosis. In fact, it was the right decision, the right thing to do.

During the next hour, I worked like crazy to save Eleanor's life. She lived, but suffered a stroke. She couldn't move her right side as a result of my medicine. I explained to her and to her family what had happened. Eleanor would need years of rehabilitation. I confronted tears, questions, and a volley of accusations from her husband. Yes, it was the medicine. Yes, it was my decision to use the medicine. With her left hand, Eleanor waved her family into silence. She grasped my arm, and in slurred, dense speech said: "You did your best, what you thought was right. Thank you for saving my life." Slowly, in the years since then I have come to understand that, however difficult, both of us did the right thing that day.

Teaching you to do the right thing is happily not always so dramatic, though unfailingly interesting. Last year, you came home from school one day long-faced and tearful. A boy at school was taunting you about your eyes. I had never thought it necessary to tell you the obvious: Being an Asian kid in a northern Vermont public school does not put you in the majority. In fact, you and your little brother are the only two Asians in the entire school.

You asked, "What should I do? He is mean. He teases me about my *eyes!*" My reflexive male reply was, (a) You should flatten him, or (b) I will flatten him for you. Your mother, always wise, suggested a different approach: Mull it over for a few days. You decide how you would like to deal with him. If, after a lot of thought, you can't resolve the problem, you can talk with us again and we will help you.

After holding our breath for several days, we finally asked you how things were going. "Yeah," you said, "he was teasing me about having

'Chink' eyes. I told him that he was wrong. I don't have 'Chink' eyes. I have Korean eyes. And I told him not to tease me anymore because it hurt my feelings. He hasn't teased me since."

A couple of days later when I was driving you to school, you pointed out the perpetrator. "There he is," you told me matter-of-factly. He was, in fact, the only black child in a school of 218 white kids and two Asian kids. His reasons for judging your different appearance were thus obvious. You and Zac have since become good friends. You have a bond between you that your schoolmates will never understand. You have done the right thing.

In the end, I wish I could tell you that in America there is lots of encouragement for doing the right thing. There isn't. Television, the movies, and newspapers rarely describe those who do the right thing. Instead, they intentionally omit or minimize such quiet, but monumental stories. The vast majority of the people we read or hear about are not leaders who choose to do the right thing. They are not your mother. They are not you. As your mother once told me, "What we are being shown of ourselves is not who we are." And if we start to believe what we see and hear, it becomes somehow OK to do less than the right thing.

This is the devil's work, an illusion you must muddle through to see what really is. Every once in a while, I hope you can recall some of the stories I have told, and others of people struggling with these difficult choices. Build upon them if you can. Enlarge them with stories of your own.

We all struggle with doing the right thing. We do it simply, courageously, and daily. We do it knowing that doing the right thing is, in the end, the only thing.

With my thanks to Spike Lee,
I love you,
Dad

The call came on a Wednesday night early in Beatrice's sophomore year, the phone ringing in the girls' dormitory, her mind still occupied with a term paper due the next day. Her boyfriend's voice on the phone was muffled: He was crying. Then, when he told her he had AIDS, she was crying, too, loud enough for her roommate to rush down the hall to see what was the matter. In those few moments, the world changed utterly. AIDS was no longer just a word, but a vivid description of a nineteen-year-old girl's future.

In the eight years since a test confirmed that Beatrice was HIV positive, she has learned much about loving life, and loving herself. She also has discovered that she has much to teach others, like her six-year-old niece and namesake, to whom this letter is addressed. Beatrice wrote the letter longhand, sitting on the deck of the split-level house in Spottsylvania, Virginia, which she shares with three cats, two dogs, and her husband, Chris. "I believe that ultimately we are not remembered by our acts but by how we loved," she says.

Dear Beatrice:

I think of the look on your face when you tell me that you love me. I hear your laughter as we play together. When I think of these moments, they are a sad reminder that I will have to leave you someday, maybe soon. They remind me that I have AIDS.

We share the same name. I pray we won't share the same fate. I know that it's unrealistic for me to expect that you will always follow my advice. So I offer you my story and hope that it will guide you as you make choices in your life. Even though I may seem perfect to you now, I do have regrets. Some things I regret I could not have changed, while others I wish I had done differently.

I regret my lost childhood. The memories are snapshots with no sequence or narration: A plate flying past me across the room. Standing at the back door of our house crying because I knew that I had to leave. Cowering in a corner, scolding myself for not being stronger. Being

"Regret can be your teacher."
BEATRICE VON GUGGENBERG KERR

Beatrice von Guggenberg Kerr and her niece and namesake, Beatrice

afraid and lonely, feeling blameworthy, unloved. I don't remember any laughter or playfulness. I grew up too fast.

When I was a teenager, I worried so much about what other people thought of me. I thought that I wasn't pretty enough, smart enough or popular enough. On my sixteenth birthday, I went to visit a friend, thinking that she had simply invited me to stop by. I didn't realize that I was actually arriving late to my own surprise birthday party. The dinner had become cold. My friends were livid and refused to speak to me. I remember tearfully apologizing, stricken with fear that I could lose all my friends over this event. My need to belong overwhelmed my feeling of betrayal over their selfish anger. I wish that I had believed in myself.

At eighteen, I thought I had found my salvation in love. I began to date Tadd, a young man who showed me love and affection. I would have given him the world. We became lovers. I knew something about sexually transmitted diseases but I thought our love provided all the protection we needed. I began taking birth control pills and one day said to Tadd, "We don't need to use condoms anymore." A year later, Tadd called and told me that he had just been diagnosed with AIDS— I never found out how he got it. How could our seemingly minor decision to stop using condoms end our lives like this? Eight months later, Tadd was dead and I was left HIV positive, frightened and alone.

My mother and father said that AIDS is a punishment from God. I heard other people say that people with AIDS deserve it because of their immoral lifestyles. Still others were afraid to come near me or to touch me for fear of infection. I regret the intolerance that exists in this world. Mostly, I regret that I accepted it. I even laughed right along with people when they told cruel jokes about people with AIDS. I would laugh and then excuse myself to the bathroom and cry.

I wanted to die. I didn't think that anyone could ever love me, not even God. The shame I felt was killing me.

Finally, I decided to try joining an AIDS support group. When I arrived, I found a close-knit and welcoming group of diverse people: a Catholic nun, a young marine, a couple of gay men, a young mother, a middle-aged woman. All were either infected or closely affected by AIDS. They accepted me without question. We hugged, cried together, supported one another. I discovered unconditional love. They became my second family. This was the first time I realized that my regrets did not have to paralyze me. I knew that I could shape my life and make it beautiful.

I also found strength within me that I never knew existed. I began to fight intolerance by educating people about AIDS. At first, I was scared. But whenever I would get in front of a group and say the words "I have AIDS," I felt a new sense of strength and purpose. Sometimes, I picture you, a few years older, sitting in that audience and then I know that all the fear in the world wouldn't stop me from trying to save your life.

Over the years I have come to peace in my relationship with your grandma and grandpa. Don't blame them for the hurtful things they have said and done. You see, they love me and all of their family very much. They can't understand how something this awful could happen to their baby, their youngest daughter. Your grandpa and grandma said that the reason for my AIDS is that God is punishing me. They hope that if only I ask for forgiveness, maybe God will give me a miracle by taking this disease away. I hope one day they will understand that God has already given me a miracle. I have lived more in the eight years since I was diagnosed with HIV than in all the nineteen years before.

Something magical has happened in my life: Every day, every moment is a gift. I'll never forget the first time this feeling struck me. I walked outside one September morning and marveled at what I saw. There were brilliant shades of yellow, red, and orange all mixed together. Then I smelled that crisp, leafy aroma of autumn. It was as if I had experienced fall for the first time. I guess that it had been so long since I felt alive that I forgot about the beauty that exists in life. Sometimes I watch you as you look up at the sky or into your father's eyes, and I know that you feel that same sense of gratefulness and wonder.

As I reach the autumn of my life, I sometimes become frightened. I don't know what the future might bring. Will it be filled with losses and regrets? As I look forward, my fear is balanced by knowing that my regrets have molded me and given me the strength to change my life for the better. It is because I have coped with past regret that I now know my future will bring me many gifts, not only losses. Regret has led me to hope.

I hope you will have few regrets in life. Even more, I hope you will learn to see regrets as opportunities to make positive changes. Regret can be your teacher, as it has been for me. I hope that you will use those lessons to mold yourself a beautiful, love-filled life.

I will always be with you.
With All My Love,
Aunt Beatrice

"It was important for me to accept
the kind of 'flower' I was."
CARLA MARSHALL

Carla Marshall with Matthew Tijerina

Every time she smells a fresh tomato, Carla Marshall thinks of summers with her grandmother, a small-boned woman in a large, blue-and-white-checked bonnet, whose lush garden yielded enough okra and green beans and fresh peas to feed seven children. "Weeds did not grow there," Marshall says. The love of horticulture she absorbed during those childhood years remains a central force in her life: Six years ago, she founded the Green Classroom, turning a 10,000-square-foot lot across from Becker Elementary School in Austin, Texas, into a wonderland of gardens, complete with a waterfall and "aqua culture" pond.

In the Green Classroom, students grow vegetables for market, study a variety of different cultures, and even practice their ABCs—the "alphabet" garden includes a flower for every letter. Most of all, they learn that plants, like people, require care and nourishment to grow. Matthew Tijerina, ten, an avid horticulturalist and champion zucchini grower, has been turning the soil under Marshall's watchful eye ever since he was in kindergarten.

Dear Matthew:

This morning I saw the first small, green leaves of the tomato plant spreading out to catch the dew. Just a few weeks ago, we planted the tiny seeds together in the garden. That small but sturdy plant, reaching for light, absorbing moisture, spreading its hairy roots, reminded me of you. No, I don't mean you look like a tomato plant. But it's been fun to watch you grow, stretch, and establish roots.

In the same way you help your plants grow in your garden here at school, your family, teachers, and friends can help you grow stronger. My wish is that in growing, you become a strong and vibrant combination of all the plants we have grown together: the softness of the scented geranium, the bright color of amaryllis, and the unusually sharp, vibrant beauty of the artichoke.

Have you noticed that no two plants are exactly alike? Each is unique—a different color, different leaves. Some are short, some soft, some rough, some pretty, some funny-looking. Some crawl along the ground; some reach for the sky.

As you grow up, you'll have friends who you might think are smarter or more handsome or happier than you can ever be. Be careful of those feelings. Many years ago, I learned an important lesson about comparing myself to others. I was at a party and my boyfriend at the time was talking with a beautiful girl. She had a flawless complexion and bright pink cheeks. To me, my skin looked sallow in comparison. She had a laugh that sounded like sleigh bells. I was sure mine was like a horse snorting. I knew this girl had done many exciting things, and my own life was dull and boring. She seemed to be everything I was not.

I went into another room all alone and began to cry. When my boyfriend came to find me, I told him through great, heaving sobs that this girl was so beautiful and smart and perfect, and he could never be happy with someone as dull as me. In my frustration I blurted out, "I'll never be like her!" and began to cry even more. But he said, "You're right! You will only be you. That is all you can ever be. Stop trying to copy someone else. Love who you are. I do."

Though at first I thought my heart would break, it wasn't long before I realized he was right. I needed to accept the kind of "flower" I was, instead of trying to turn myself into a rose when I was a perfectly good, vibrant zinnia. I want so much for you to accept yourself and love who you are. Doing so is one of the very hardest things, but if you don't do it, it becomes difficult to be loved by others, because deep inside you are unhappy and dissatisfied.

Do you remember when you were in kindergarten and everyone's squash plants grew except yours? For some reason, your plant was very small—so small we had to look closely to see it at all. I know you must remember, because when we had the Harvest Festival in the Green Classroom at the end of the year, you won first prize for the biggest zucchini. That zucchini grew at its own pace, and in its own time it became a prize-winning, beautiful plant.

As you grow, your family and teachers will want you to develop at a pace they think is right. For example, they will be disappointed if you have trouble with reading or math, and will compare you with others. They want you to have these skills for good reasons: They are tools for living and competing in a very competitive world. But always remember how slowly that zucchini grew and what a prize-winner it became. Always try to do your best, and let that be your guide. The voice inside your head and your heart will let you know when you're really trying or when you're goofing off.

I'm going to tell you a secret about how slowly I grew: When I was in school, other kids made fun of me because I was so tall and skinny. One time in elementary school, the school nurse weighed everyone and measured their height. But the worst part came when we returned to class and had to call out our measurements in front of the class. I was the tallest, which seemed embarrassing enough, but I also weighed the least. I'll never forget how everyone laughed at me.

Then, a number of years later, something very surprising happened. I was hired as a high-fashion model, wearing beautiful, expensive clothing and getting paid for it! Suddenly, all the things I hated about myself—my skinny legs, my neck as long as a flamingo's—were considered "beautiful." And the funniest part was that I felt "short" next to many of the other models. So it is a very funny world when you believe in the picture of yourself reflected by others.

My body wasn't the only thing slow to develop. I seemed to be slow in every way. I didn't begin college until I was in my forties. I didn't meet my husband until that same age. I didn't find the work I love—the Green Classroom—until I was almost fifty! Everyone else seemed to have accomplished those things long before. Sometimes I thought there was something very wrong with me.

Then, when I was twenty-eight, I saved my money to go to Europe for a one-month vacation. The flight landed in the tiny European country of Luxembourg, where I checked into a youth hostel. As I explored, I loved the old buildings, the different food; it was all so mysterious and enchanting. I decided to extend my month's stay, and before I knew it, a year had passed and I had traveled all over Europe, loving every minute. There was something about traveling that allowed me, for the first time, to move at my own pace and to discover new things about myself. I learned that there was nothing wrong with me or my timing. And I met so many brilliant and fascinating people who accepted me, flamingo neck and all!

So, Matthew, my hope for you is that you can find your own way to grow and blossom. You are wonderful, special, and unique. You can grow strong in your own way by listening to that voice inside and caring about the earth that nourishes you. And as you grow, keep your connection with Nature, and continue to grow the biggest zucchini!

With great affection,
Carla Marshall

At fourteen, most girls are thinking about boys, homework, swim meets, and what to wear to the next party. Angela Putman had something else on her mind: She was pregnant. In a single year, Angela grew up fast, her childhood tempered by adult decisions and adult emotions, by profound lessons in responsibility, courage — and grief.

Years later, telling her story to her future husband, K. C. Richardson, Angela worried that he would reject her. Instead, he expressed wonder at "the change that God can make in people's lives." "He is incredibly accepting," she says. The couple now lives near Johnson City, Tennessee, where Angela works at Girls, Inc., drawing upon her own experience to counsel teenagers like Michelle Hairston, fifteen.

Dear Michelle:

When I was your age, I was controlled by fear. Fear of rejection. Fear of not being popular. At thirteen I moved to a new town and school. I had to make new friends in a small community where everyone had grown up together. I was so anxious to have friends that I was not true to myself. Coming from a small, private Christian school, I was flattered by the attention I received from the boys at my new school. At the end of eighth grade I began to date a guy who was popular. I had never really dated anyone seriously, and I was unprepared for dealing with the pressure he put on me to make sex a part of our relationship. I was afraid of losing my boyfriend, with whom I was sure I was in love. Eventually my fear won out and I gave in. And so at fourteen, I was no longer a virgin. Later, I found out that I was pregnant.

Looking back, it's amazing that I never felt fear about what the consequences of my actions might be. But those consequences were so much more than I might have imagined. I was raised in a Christian home. My father was a minister at a local church. I knew right from wrong. Yet I allowed fear to sway me from the principles I held.

Suddenly, the fear of losing friends and my boyfriend seemed so insignificant. I was faced with adult concerns much deeper than wanting to be liked and accepted by those at school. As I thought about how

"I ask myself this question: Is this something
I will be proud of in the future?"
ANGELA PUTMAN RICHARDSON

Angela Putman Richardson with student Michelle Hairston

people would respond to my situation, I knew what I had to do. I remembered my dad telling the story of a girl named Mary who, when she found out she was pregnant, went before the whole church and told them about it. I was very compelled by that story. And I realized that true acceptance from my church family would come best through openness and complete honesty. So a few days after I found out I was pregnant and told my parents, I made plans to go before the church.

As the day approached, I began to experience serious fear. It seemed that our whole family was afraid. Well, the day finally arrived, and when the time came for me to go forward I stood up and walked to the front, and I began to cry. My father was not preaching that Sunday. A close family friend had taken over for him in that time of extreme stress. When he saw that I was crying too hard to talk, he turned to the congregation and said, "Angela has come forward to say that she has sinned and she wants to repent." The congregation was sympathetic, but they didn't understand right away what was going on. So my dad came forward and explained the situation to them. I was crying too hard to speak.

God really encouraged me that day—through His people. Those wonderful people were so accepting and loving. I sat on the front pew and after church was over they rushed to me and hugged me and told me they loved me. Truly they were a gift from God. From that day on, I never felt afraid or embarrassed to go to church. I had made a mistake, but God was going to use it for my good. He was going to help me live through the consequences and help me become a better person because of it.

The next year was the most difficult in my life. I decided, against the wishes of many people, to give my baby up for adoption rather than to have an abortion or to keep the baby. Throughout the months of my pregnancy, my boyfriend and I struggled in trying to choose a good family. During my pregnancy I gained a lot of weight and was forced to give up playing sports and being a cheerleader. I also experienced a real sense of separation from my peers. You can probably imagine what it was like for a fourteen-year-old girl to walk through a mall or restaurant obviously pregnant. Yet through it all, I felt a real peace about the decisions I was making. I also felt closeness to God, and it was this that carried me through this difficult time.

I began to see the foolishness of my earlier attitudes and actions. I spent a lot of time thinking about the way in which I had previously made decisions. And I determined that from that point on I would ask myself a question before making decisions: "Is this something that I will be proud of in the future?" That question helped me to put things into perspective. You see, the people I had allowed to influence me weren't even going to be a part of my life five years later. And I alone was the one who would have to take responsibility for the decisions I made. Thinking in those terms helped me to realize that my decisions had to be about what was best for me and my future, not about fitting in with others.

One of the reasons I decided to give my baby up for adoption was because I wanted desperately to redeem my mistake in some way. I knew that I couldn't change the past, but I also realized that from then on I needed to be true to my convictions. I felt that I couldn't provide a good home at such a young age, and I knew God wouldn't condone an abortion.

I can honestly say that that was the most heart-wrenching decision I have ever had to make. Many times I desperately wanted to change my mind. But I knew that to do so would be selfish. I knew that my child deserved a strong family who would give so much love. It helped to be a part of the choosing of a couple, and to know that they also were anxiously awaiting the birth of my baby.

The time finally came for the baby to be born. The due date arrived, and passed. One week later, Ashley Rose was born, on March 17, 1986. She was more beautiful than I could have imagined. The adoptive family was notified of her birth and traveled to come and see her. If I thought that I had felt anguish before Ashley was born, there was no comparison to the heartbreak that followed her birth.

As the time arrived to give her to her new parents, the doctors began to see some problems with her health. Within a few days, she had dramatically declined. The doctors determined that her heart had not developed properly and that open-heart surgery would be required. Several different procedures were attempted, but ultimately it was clear that Ashley would not survive. Ashley Rose died on March 24, 1986. She lived one week.

Many times I question why. But as I remember a life controlled by fear, I see the tremendous good that came out of the short life of Ashley Rose. She was such a special, special little baby. She touched so many in her life and in her death.

I still struggle with fear of rejection, and I find that I still have a difficult time trusting those who are close to me. But now I think long and hard about the decisions I make, and I listen closely to my conscience. I have learned to seek the counsel of those who love me.

It is natural for a person to experience some fear. The key, I believe, is to not give in to it. My wrong decision did not affect only myself. It affected my family, my friends, and many others around me. So many times we do not realize that our lives are connected to the lives of others. My decision resulted in my pregnancy, in embarrassment, in judgment of my family by other people, and in rejection by my peers: ironically, the very thing I was so afraid of.

Michelle, as I watch you from day to day, I am consistently impressed by your strength and independence. But I also see the sacrifices you must make in order to be true to yourself. I want to encourage you to stand firm even if it becomes more difficult to do so as you grow older. Do not allow the fear of rejection to overcome your desire to live your life in a way you can be proud of. Don't allow others to tear down your belief in yourself. Hold your head up a little bit higher. You really will be able to look back on these years with pride.

Love,
Angela

"You were so brave, the people were so loving,
and it was a very wise thing to do."
PASTOR BILL PUTMAN

Bill Putman

Pastor Bill Putman, executive director of the Montana Christian Evangelizing Association and minister of the Kings Christian Church in Missoula, is Angela Richardson's father. He will never forget the words his daughter spoke to him in the middle of the night eleven years ago, or the changes her revelation and her courage brought to all their lives. The message he took from their experience: "There can be redemption after failure. That is what we learned and how the church treated us. We have been wonderfully accepted." He and his wife, Bobbi, have four other children.

To my daughter Angela:

I suppose that looking back is painful to many people, but because of how you have faced the issues of your life, looking back brings me joy and thanksgiving. I remember the night when you slipped into our bedroom at two o'clock in the morning. I was suddenly wide awake at your words: "Daddy, please don't hate me! I'm pregnant!" I remember the pain and the emotions that flooded over me, and the questions and worries that shook me to the core: "What did I do wrong?" "Why would you do this to me?" "Didn't I teach you better?" "Now I'll have to leave my job as a pastor."

Do you remember your fear of telling me? Of wondering how Mom and I would take the news? I'm so glad that we were able to pull you in between us and say, "Oh, Angela, of course we'll forgive you. We love you. We'll get through this together."

Angela, that night I wanted both to shake you and to hug you. I wanted to spank you and hold you in my arms. The crisis of that moment brought me the greatest challenge of my life. But my pain soon turned to pride. I watched a little girl become a full-grown woman almost overnight. I watched you face the consequences of your behavior and stand tall.

I couldn't fully understand when you said, "I am going to step forward in church tomorrow, tell people what I've done and ask forgiveness." You were so brave, and the people were so loving, and it was a very wise thing to do. It was so difficult for us to turn the responsibility of the decisions over to you and the boy, to watch you deal with him, and his parents, and the problems of what to do with the coming baby. Until you, too, have a teenager, you will never fully understand how your children's failure affects your feelings about yourself. It's so easy as a parent to take the blame for what your children do, to feel defeated.

The pain I felt helped me take a different look at your mom and at the other kids. I watched your mother ignore her own personal needs, becoming the glue that held us together as a family. I watched your brother and sisters, grandparents, aunts, and uncles rally around you when some of your friends rejected you. The close family I had always wanted actually became a reality.

Angela, it's so easy to give people platitudes and simple answers. But when it's your turn to face the same problems, living up to those answers is hard to do. I remember a night that proved to be "one of those" for me. I came home from work and heard you and Mom in the bedroom. I walked to the door and heard you crying out, "Oh, Mom, if I could only go back six months, this wouldn't have happened." I walked into the room and said something I had said before: "Angela, you can't go back, but because of Jesus Christ, you can start over."

I watched you turn your back on your past and face day by day the hundreds of decisions you had to make. I watched you decide not to abort your baby: "Dad, I made one mistake, I'm not going to make another," you said. I watched you continue in school and never miss one day until our baby Ashley was born. I knew that if Mom and I made the decisions for you, they might not be ones you could live with. I'm so glad we let you decide. You did great.

Sis, I watched you suffer when Ashley died after just one week of life. The pain and loss you carried broke my heart. I saw your loneliness when the boy abandoned you and left us with the doctor bills, your struggling to go through the grief and build a future for yourself.

Because of the many doctor bills, Mom and I couldn't help you with college. Yet we watched you work to accomplish one goal after the other. You finished high school, got your undergraduate degree, and now have a master's in education, too. You struggled to find just the right person to share your life and dreams with.

Thank you for allowing me to be a part of your life. The difficulties we faced together strengthened my faith and allowed our disjointed family to be bound together. I'm so glad that God allowed me to be your birth father and that you have allowed me to be your friend.

Sis, I love you.
Dad

"We all cope with life in different ways, take, pass,
and sometimes fail tests, swim our way through
in smooth and rough water."
ARVONNE FRASER

Arvonne Fraser and granddaughter Allison

She is a tiny woman with big passions, fierce in her convictions, expansive in her love for her children and grandchildren, sobered by her share of loss—larger than most. Arvonne Fraser was born independent, or so it sometimes seems to her, growing up on a farm outside Lamberton, Minnesota, listening to her mother's exhortation, "Always be able to support yourself." In 1962, she left her career behind, moving to Washington as a congressman's wife, but soon was reading Betty Friedan, dubbing her newly formed women's group "The Nameless Sisterhood," setting up a Washington chapter of Women's Equity Action League. In time, she took her efforts worldwide, as a Jimmy Carter appointee to the Agency for International Development, and then as a Humphrey Institute fellow, founding the International Women's Rights Action Watch.

Now seventy, Fraser sips coffee on the big screened porch at the summer house, gazes out at the blue river water beyond the trees, smokes a cigarette, taps at her computer. She has survived successes and mistakes, outlived two daughters, built a life with her husband and her family that is deep and long-lasting, a richly woven fabric to share with her twelve-year-old granddaughter, Allison. "It's nice to get old and say what you really think," she told a newspaper reporter. "Of course, most people think I've been doing that for years."

Dear Allison,

Remember last summer when you swam clear across the river? Your mother, aunts and uncles all had done it in their time, and bragged about it. Pick a weekday, they said, when hardly any boats are out and there's no wind, a blue-sky day, with high, fluffy clouds. I will row the boat beside you and somebody else will be the watcher, ready to throw you a lifejacket if you get too tired.

You never came close to needing a lifejacket. You had grown a lot in one year, had stronger legs, longer feet. None of the boys on the beach had made that swim yet, so you were doubly challenged. About fifty feet past Grandpa's sailboat, your grim, worried look vanished and your strokes got smoother. Nobody had to tell you to turn on your back, rest a bit, and see how far you had traveled. New experiences can be frightening, but this was your day. If I live to be 100 (and you and I both may) I'll never forget the sight of you, all that long blond hair plastered against your head, your sunburned nose and a great grin as you came up for breath. Like a ballet dancer.

Remembering your traumatic birth, that fifty-mile rush in an ambulance to a Chicago hospital's neonatal wing, I said to myself that it was a miracle. Other newborns were no bigger than coffee cans. You were the nine-pounder, my first grandchild, born large and apparently full of determination. The first time I saw you, I felt like I was in a spaceship full of babies, all of you hooked up to machines, monitors registering wavy green lines.

Has your mother told you all this? I'm not sure she can without crying all over again. Having her two sisters die was bad enough. Worrying that you would die, too, is more than she can talk about easily. Dealing with death too often is probably why she eats too much and is a little tougher than most mothers. I know it's why I still smoke, so forgive me. We all cope with life in different ways, take, pass and sometimes fail tests, swim our way through in smooth and rough water.

One Saturday night after you were released from the hospital, your mom called to ask if I would make you a little patchwork quilt out of my fabric scraps. At last I can do something, I thought, reminding myself of what our pediatrician friend said the day after you were born: "Babies are very resilient. They mend amazingly well." The quilt needed black and white, contrasting textures, bright colors to stimulate your eyes and your sense of touch. And a really crazy quilt it still is, not so colorful now after hundreds of washings. Maybe you should put it away for your children and grandchildren. They'd like it, I'm sure, and you can tell them your story and give them advice like I'm giving you.

One story you might tell them is the one about your great-great-great-grandmother finding the bear on the other side of the bush when she was out picking berries. You might add a new ending, too: Don't fight over berries with a bear. Just walk away quietly to another bush.

Walking away from fights you can't win is a good idea, but don't give up something you feel strongly about without at least discussing it. I walked away from my bad first marriage. I hated to admit I had made a mistake and I did a lot of thinking—something I should have done before I married. We all make mistakes. Learning to admit them is the hard part.

You need to do a lot of talking and thinking before you decide you're willing to spend the rest of your life with someone. Before we married, Grandpa and I argued about whether there could be two captains of a ship. I argued for co-captains, dividing up the work. He said later he decided to marry me because he knew I'd fit in at the river, but we all know he still likes to argue and discuss things with me.

Your mom brought your father out to the river before she married him, too. He wouldn't stay for dinner that first time. Our big family, with Grandpa and I both in politics, and everybody saying what they thought, probably scared him.

Have you ever heard the saying "Different folks, different strokes"? Like families, people are different, and like different ways of living and working. Having no road and no TV at the river house bothers some people: They don't come a second time. We like family and friends coming and going, but also sitting quietly in the rocking chairs on the porch on lazy afternoons, looking out at the water and the woods.

Storms can be exciting, too. Remember how scared you and Willie were that first summer you stayed alone with us? But you soon found in the thunder and lightning, the rushing around to lock all the banging windows when that first big gust of wind and rain comes, a new kind of excitement. Well, life is like that: frightening and exciting, full of stormy and bright days. The trick is learning to deal with both.

"Use your head, girl," my mother used to say. I sometimes think of my head as my special, private room. There I can do what I want, think about terrible or good things, create imaginary worlds, test out ideas and try to anticipate and solve problems.

We don't know nearly as much about the mind as about the body. Some people are afraid of what's in their heads. Terrible thoughts and ideas overwhelm them. When we lived in Washington and President Kennedy was killed, the children asked why. I told them the person who killed him was sick in his head and afterwards they talked about "sickheads."

I hope your generation will discover the causes and cures for mental illness. Your mother's younger sister became increasingly depressed after she saw her older sister, Annie, killed crossing the street. Once, when she was feeling bad, I asked her what she thought was good about herself. "I'm nice to people," she said. She was. For years she sent a good part of her allowance to an organization that supported poor kids overseas. But she couldn't see a future, always wanted to do everything too fast, like going to school when she was four, and the university at sixteen. She ultimately committed suicide, as you know. So beautiful and bright she was, but those gorgeous, sad brown eyes.

You're not sad, and you have so many great years ahead of you, so many rivers to swim. Take a piece of paper. Fold it in two. On the left side, write down all the things you'd like to do or learn before you're 100. On the right side write down things not to do, and why you shouldn't do them.

Has your mom told you the story about the time she sneaked off to the little store and bought candy and hid some of it in a tree? When she went back to get the candy, ants were swarming all over it. You learned last summer not to wear shorts in the woods: poison ivy! You must have other "don'ts" to put on the list, things that you've learned through bad experiences.

Grandpa may someday warn you about the sign over the courtroom door, "If you tell the truth, you don't have to remember what you said." It's hard to remember lies. Making the list of things you want to do is more fun. What mountains would you like to climb? What places do you want to see? Think big. Never in my wildest dreams, as a young farm girl, did I ever think I'd be traveling all over the world as part of my work, but it happened. I always knew I wanted children and grandchildren as well as work, and money of my own. My mother made me take typing in school so I would always be able to support myself. She knew that women can't depend on a rich Prince Charming to come along and take care of them.

Writing all this also made me think of another list you could make, a "why?" list. Write down all the things you wonder about and want answers to. I've still got plenty of questions I want answered. Bring your lists along when you come this summer, and maybe we can get Grandpa in this game, too. I don't think I'll put swimming across the river on my "to do" list. I'd rather row the boat and watch you.

Love,
Grandma Arvonne

"If one language is good, two is even better."
VICTOR HERNÁNDEZ CRUZ

Victor Hernández Cruz and daughter Rosa Kairi Cruz

This is what the poet Victor Hernández Cruz sees from the balcony of his house in Aguas Buenas, Puerto Rico: the town spread out below, little houses painted in pale colors, the cross on the church, green mountains in the distance. He likes to lie in the hammock on the balcony and read, sometimes in English, sometimes in Spanish. By the time he was sixteen, Cruz was spinning images together, crafting melodic lines of feeling and intellect, songs out of words. "The urge to write was inside of me," he says. "Poetry is not just a mental thing, but a biological thing, too, something that goes through the whole body."

The Caribbean is a good place to write a poem. Sounds travel more easily there, Cruz says, morning sounds, the sound of roosters, of conversations, of insects and animals. Smells, too: fresh coffee, ocean, fruit trees. He wrote this letter in the morning, sitting on the balcony, thinking of his sixteen-year-old daughter, Rosa Kairi Cruz, and of what, of this rich life, he can sing to her.

Dear Kairi:

I am looking forward to your visit to the island. It has become a tradition for you to come down here from your home in San Francisco in the summer. Down here people love traditions, that's why each town celebrates the day of its patron saint. This year, your visit is timed so that you can observe three days of the festival here in Aguas Buenas. You will see the procession on the first day, when they carry La Virgen de Monserrate, the black Virgin, through the streets, with candles and singing.

It has been hot and humid, but we are lucky to have the trees, mountains and beaches to make it all bearable. The original inhabitants of the island knew how to live in this climate. They made their dwellings, known as *yucayeyes*, by the cool current of a river. They divided the work up, and had everything in balance. Nowadays there're too many cars and too much concrete. When you come, I want to take you to the mountains, to some high elevations where you can see beautiful panoramas and get inspired to paint. Or perhaps you will start singing without knowing it and without any effort.

When the Spaniards saw these mountains in 1493, they thought they were in Paradise. It was a whole different way of living from what they were used to. When you come this summer, we could visit little towns in the mountains. Each town is known for a different fruit. Aguas Buenas is the town of *mameyes*, a native fruit. Mayagüez is known for its juicy and abundant mangoes and so on. In each place, we could talk to local people and learn the history that they know. There still is a lot of song here, and I would like you to hear songs that go along with guitars and songs that go along with drums.

Your grandmother wants to teach you how to cook with yucca and plantains, delicious dishes created during the last five hundred years as the food of the native Indians, Spain, and Africa have come together. I will teach you how to separate the ingredients, identifying their place of origin and how they got to this Caribbean island, then put them all together again. You can do this with music and dance also. It's like taking fibers apart, seeing each color separately, then bringing them back together to see the beauty that they form. By knowing those connections you will know your history.

You and your cousin Lisa, and Moddy, and all your other friends down here could be out on the street playing a game, and in your mind, like a camera, you could have a picture, a bird's-eye view of all the Caribbean islands and all the little streets, the singing of a continent made of islands. Streets connected to mountains, mountains connected to sandy beaches, surrounded by the immense ocean which is our bridge to the rest of the world. You will then know exactly where you are standing. And if you know where you are standing, you will know how to walk; you will feel how everything moves through you, and from you out to embrace everything on the earth. Here is a poem that I have written especially for you:

> *To Kairi*
> *Are you speaking Spanish?*
> *So that next time you come*
> *You can talk with your*
> *Girlfriends*
> *Remember the games where*

You clap your hands and sing,
As if the words were in the palms.
If the language where you are is English
But in your house they sometimes
Speak Spanish—
It sounds like something warm and round
It sounds of love,
Spanish like feathers in air
Romantic.
I think of the two languages
I write in both
In one I find something
that I can't find in the other
I make little bridges
I can walk across the bridge
All day long.
To me Spanish seems to be round and vegetable
English is vertical and goes
Straight up into the air
Like a cylinder pipe.
In English it is like being inside walls.
Spanish is outdoors and circles.
When I go outside I see words
Walking around the streets—
Spanish letters have cotton
At the tips so they don't bang
into the letters next to them
To make ugly sounds—.
They dress in fresh cotton
To make words danse valse
Under orange trees.
Look at a map of the Caribbean
In Cuba, Puerto Rico and Santo Domingo
People speak in Spanish.
Look now to where Mexico begins
Keep going down all of Central America

And on to South America.
All those countries sing in Spanish—.
So you should practice your Spanish
Think of all the countries you can
Speak it in.
If one language is good
Two is better
Don't forget your Spanish
Next time you are down here
I'll take you by the hands
And in Spanish you can
Like for the very first time—
Tell me the names of things.

Love *siempre,*
Victor Hernández Cruz

John Winthrop is a South Carolina tree farmer, a highly successful money manager, a transplanted New Englander, and the direct descendant of another John Winthrop—founder of the city of Boston. But most of all he is, at fifty-nine, the father of a fourth son born later in life, when the passage of time is more vivid, the importance of filling it wisely more apparent. Of Edward Field Winthrop, his nine-year-old son from a second marriage, Winthrop says, "I want him to count on me each morning when I take him to school, to count on me when I put him to bed at night."

The day "Teddy" was born, Winthrop wrote him a letter, and later, another one, beginning a tradition of gifts from father to son, a legacy of thoughts and yearnings and recollections, a place to talk quietly about the important things, like dreams, and sports, and trees, and the fact that life cannot continue forever.

Dear Teddy:

Your awareness of the end of life took shape on this day. You had been watching a video, a cleverly orchestrated story about a baby dinosaur who lost his mother and father. The story described how the baby missed his mother, but that her soul would never leave him as he grew older.

Coincidentally, Joe Frazer, a black man and dear friend of ours here in South Carolina, died recently. I let you know how I would miss him and allowed you to come with me as I left some flowers with his widow.

You have asked me many times about my wrinkles and about whether or not I would leave you. On the way back to Charleston that afternoon, many of these thoughts built up inside you—you insisted on knowing where your grandparents were, and then you asked again, with greater urgency, whether I would leave you.

Feeling it was best to be honest as we drove along, I told you, as you sat in your mother's lap beside me, that I might have to leave you someday, but our souls would always be together. It was difficult for me to say exactly where our souls would be, but I believed all of us would be in heaven together someday. All this was a long ways away, I explained.

"I told you I might have to leave you someday,
but that our souls would always be together."
JOHN WINTHROP

John Winthrop and son Ted

Tears came into your eyes during the next part of our talk. I will always remember it. "I want to hold on tight to you," you said, and, after a pause, "I want to go to heaven and sleep with you there." Then you said that your feelings were hurt, and you cried some more.

It made me put myself in your shoes and think back, way back in time, when I lost my grandfather—"Bapa" we used to call him. Bapa was afflicted with deafness, but he found time nearly every day to come over and play with his grandchildren in Manchester, Massachusetts.

We bonded at an early age. Bapa let his three grandsons climb up on him, play ball with him. He would tell stories and then draw pictures of various wild animals who had spectacular adventures.

I'll never forget the stories he told about an adventurous mouse named Johnnie Mouse. Nor the pictures he drew of people living inside a whale or a lion, having been swallowed whole. They made a lifelong impression on me. The people in the stories and in the pictures were always happy. And your great-grandfather made your father happy, very happy, always.

In like manner, you and I have bonded, just as I did with your brothers when they were young. We did all the usual things fathers and sons do. We played sports and told stories and worked through problems together.

Being a father in one's fifties is a little different from being a father in one's thirties. Each day must be savored; every hour must be lived fully.

I do think more about death than I did years ago. Much comfort has come to me with the knowledge that our lives are woven together despite the difference in our years. The love I feel for you is without any condition or motive. In the first hour of your life you yawned at me— clearly not a sign of respect! We were left alone together on that early morning; I'll never forget that important time of bonding. The awareness that I might not be around when you grew older made me write you letters on all kinds of subjects: why sports should be important to you; how to approach your studies; why your mother and father came to Charleston from New England; why I grow trees. These letters were written with a longing to communicate with you far into the future, even if I was not around.

Your father has been blessed with an enormously full life, even if it should end tomorrow. You, along with a very few others, have added to my journey in a significant way, more so than you will ever know. At some level you are aware of these thoughts, although we have never discussed them as fully as I am now writing about them. Each night when we say our prayers, I mention all those in your life and at the end, you always add in your own words, ". . . and let me die when Dad dies."

When you said this the first time as a five-year-old, your hands folded, it startled me. And yet it was so easy to understand. You simply wanted to share time together. This has made all the difference to me, and I am doing my best to continue to stick around for the joy of each unfolding day.

When your great-grandfather—his name was Matthew Bartlett— died, I was told very suddenly that he had gone to heaven and that I would not be seeing him again. I was devastated. The sense of loss lasted a long time for me, and for my mother, who adored him as well. The two of them used to sail together, father and daughter, off the coast of Massachusetts, when your grandmother was a little girl. I was introduced to this anonymous piece, written about a sailboat:

THE SHIP

I am standing upon the seashore. A ship at my side spreads her white sails to the morning breeze and starts for the blue ocean.

She is an object of beauty and strength, and I stand and watch her until at length she is only a speck of white cloud just where the sea and sky meet and mingle with each other. Then someone at my side exclaims, "There! She's gone."

Gone where? Gone from my sight—that is all. She is just as large in hull and mast and spar as she was when she left my side, and just as able to bear her load of living freight to the place of her destination. Her diminished size is in me, not in her.

And just at the moment when someone at my side says, "She's gone," there are other eyes watching for her coming and other voices ready to take up the glad shout, "There she comes!"

And that is dying.

These words gave me great comfort. They still give me comfort when I think about them now. Perhaps this word picture became even more comforting after my mother and my father died. You must take comfort in it as well. Someday all of us will be reunited and our souls will be together. I feel confident of that.

With love,
Dad

"Did you have some sense even then
of what it was like to be a refugee?"
MAI CONG

Mai Cong and niece Tina

In her mind's eye she can still see the Vietnamese countryside, the lush green of the bamboo trees, the bungalows and thatched-roof cottages, the people working in the rice fields. But Mai Cong is an American now. "One of these days I would want to go and visit, but my home is here," she says.

The transition was not easy. Fleeing Saigon in 1975, Cong settled in Santa Ana, California, gradually adapting to a new language, new food, and a landscape of palm trees and cactus. Now she helps others make the same journey, working as a mental health counselor for refugees in Orange County, and serving as CEO of the Vietnamese Community of Orange County, Inc. Cong's twenty-one-year-old niece, Tina (her Vietnamese name is Quynh Cong) traveled to Vietnam last summer.

My Dear Niece:

Congratulations! I can't tell you how happy I am to learn of your graduation from college. It was a real delight to read your last letter. How far you have come from the frail little girl I saw for the first time at the airport in Los Angeles, clutching at her mother's robe, fearful and lost at the end of your long journey across the Pacific.

My home was your first in the U.S.: You stayed with me in California for two weeks before going to New York to be reunited with your father, my brother, a former Vietnamese army lieutenant turned mailman. When you left, you cried so much. But during the fourteen years since, you have remained with me. I think of you every time I look at the painting you sent me, an art assignment from school, tacked up on the wall of my study.

Your painting has always exerted a strange fascination for me. There is not much else in it besides a dark blue, almost threatening sky, weighing down upon a snow-covered landscape. At the far end of the road—a stretch of chilling, silvery brightness, barely covered with a hint of icy blue—two forlorn shadows are either approaching or walking away.

I know that those figures represent you and your mother, trudging through the snow of New York in the dead of winter that year. Did you have some vague sense back then of what it was like to be a refugee? Of what it was like to be insecure even though you had found a new home? Or was it just the bleakness of your first winter in New York?

I can imagine how proud your parents must be now that you have successfully completed your undergraduate studies. I am glad that you did it, and you certainly deserve your vacation, the trip to Vietnam you wrote me about.

I can understand that your parents might be unwilling to talk about certain subjects, for example, their experiences during and after the war, experiences that are too painful for them to recall. Did you know that you and your mother were lost in the crowd of refugees and that the two of you were separated from your father in the last days of the war? Did you know that for a few years your father lived like a half-dead man, delivering mail in that big city without any news from his wife and infant child? Being born in the last year of the war, you were lucky to be spared the traumas inflicted by that terrible conflict, the longest in this century. We are all survivors.

You asked about what it was like when I left the country. I still remember vividly that day, a Sunday in April, twenty years ago. A rocket barrage had torn apart a large part of Saigon. It was chaotic. People ran through the streets frantically, like animals in a cage. Many people had already left. In the morning, I went to church, hoping that my friends might also go and I would meet them there. But the church was empty, and I sat in the deserted chapel alone, praying. Then we were told to go and spend the night at the airport. I packed a suitcase, grabbing a small iron, some French perfume and some photographs. I wanted to hold on to things that I thought would give substance to my life, however insignificant they were. I was with my mother and sister. Immediately after our plane took off the next morning, the airport was bombed. It was all over.

By the time I got to Camp Pendleton—the large refugee reception center arranged by U.S. Marines in Southern California—I felt numb and dead inside. I drew a little map of the part of Saigon where I had lived on a piece of paper, and I located my house on the map, so I would always remember it. I still thought we would be able to go back to Vietnam and resume our life as if nothing had happened. There was a war, and millions of people had died. But it had gone on for so long that it had become part of our life.

On the fifth day at the camp, I shook off my stupor and joined with other volunteers in the camp, welcoming other refugees, passing out clothes, taking turns in the mess hall. The work gave me a sense of purpose and I have volunteered ever since, to help the refugee community.

I still have that map which I drew on a scrap of paper in Camp Pendleton twenty years ago. I have never used it, and, in all likelihood, I never will.

I am reminded of an American fairy tale, "Rip Van Winkle," by Washington Irving. There is a Vietnamese legend that is similar, the story of Tu Thuc, and both involve universal themes of exile and return. I believe those stories will make quite pertinent reading for you on the eve of your departure.

In the stories, both men run away from oppressive circumstances and find themselves in supernatural settings, you know, a place where there is only delight and serenity. The United States, despite its many current problems, is still looked upon this way by many people in the world; many young people here take so much for granted. In any case, both Rip and his counterpart in the Vietnamese story eventually returned to what they thought was "home." Instead, since a day in paradise is equal to one hundred years on earth, they found themselves strangers in a strange land. In the American fairy tale, Rip resigns himself to his old town because at least he has gotten away from his wife, the impossible Dame Van Winkle, who had vanished from the scene in his absence. But Tu Thuc, the Vietnamese Rip Van Winkle, again takes off in search of the paradise he has left, and is never seen again.

No, I am not trying to discourage you from going. Why should I? You need to find your roots. But while men and women have always felt the need to go to faraway places to escape from the fears, the anxieties, the uncertainties that are the common lot of man, I believe they are searching for something that in the end can only be found within themselves, and within their community. That something is a clear sense of who we are and where we are, our true roots, our true culture, our true identity.

Even in this terrible century, we have much to be thankful for. I believe that this "winter," like the winter in your painting, will in the end yield to a new spring, with limitless possibilities.

And so, Tina, thank you for sharing with me your travel plans, and the good news about your graduation. Go, since you have to, and tell me of your experiences when you come home. In the meantime, stick to the values that are eternal, such as honesty, responsibility and loyalty, and to the ideals of life, liberty and the pursuit of happiness we all hold dear. Most of all, as a poet once said, always be true to yourself.

Love,
Mai Cong

Choices

"If you look at history, I hardly ever screw up twice
at the same thing."
BOB ASMUSSEN

Bob Asmussen and daughter Kristen

Bob Asmussen took one adoring look at his newborn daughter Kristen twelve years ago and knew his days of high-risk motorcycle antics, barhopping, and all-night parties were over. Still, he kept riding his Harley, giving it up only after a back injury forced his retirement. On a "hog," Asmussen says, "it is total freedom—beyond anything you can imagine. You are only two and a half feet from death every time you ride."

In Riverdale, Maryland, Asmussen's life has settled into a comfortable family routine—compelling, but no longer dangerous. In his spare time, the forty-seven-year-old Bell Atlantic equipment mechanic can be found coaching girls' sports at a nearby Catholic church, fishing on his 22.5-foot boat, or working on the miniature "biker town" train set—complete with pawnshop, beer joint, and go-go bar—he built in his basement. When it comes to raising kids, Asmussen says he had a good role model: his dad. "He is a good father and a good example. He never abused any of us or tried to cut us down, and he was always encouraging, which is what I've tried to be."

Kristen:

Hi, it's Dad. I want to take a few minutes of your time to give you advice it's taken me a lifetime to learn. You've heard me say it to many of the teams I have coached over the last twenty years, and now I'm saying it directly to you: "It doesn't matter how bad you screw up. What matters is how you recover."

With my teams this means in a basketball game, if you take a shot and miss, you go for the rebound. If the other team gets the rebound, you get back on defense. Don't fall to the floor pounding your fist. Don't have a tantrum while the rest of your team continues to play ball. You'll get left behind.

In baseball, some kids boot the ball trying to field it. You only know what a kid is made of *after* the mistake is made. Most will pick it up as quickly as possible and try to make a play. But some will throw their glove in the dirt while the rest of the team plays ball. That behavior usually lets teammates down at the worst time.

To make it in life you have to stay in the game.

When I was born, I was pigeon-toed. I could hardly walk. It was a screwup that wasn't my fault, but it had the same effect. I could have felt sorry for myself—I probably did; I don't remember. But there was a point in junior high school when I decided I wouldn't walk funny again. I don't now.

You know of my problems with my back. Again, not my fault, but still a problem. I've spent many months lying on the floor in pain because I couldn't get up. I have to exercise almost every day, but I know what I have to do and I adjust for it, even when the adjustment meant selling my Harley. I rode motorcycles for twenty-four years and it was extremely hard to give them up. But it was one of the adjustments I had to make to recover.

In my biker days, I don't think many people screwed up more than I did. I've ridden with guys that, like me, were so messed up that when we came to a stoplight they would forget to put their feet down. Boy does that hurt. Some of my friends are dead. I've made adjustments and tried my best to recover. They didn't make it. Actually, I guess it's called learning from your mistakes.

When I was in high school, it seems like I spent a lot of time screwing up. I got suspended for gambling once. I got suspended for fighting once. But I still graduated and went on to college for a year and a half. My high school ring is still on my right hand.

While going to college, I guess you could say I screwed up again when my girlfriend got pregnant. I don't know if my marriage to her was a screwup or not, but it ended in divorce. I learned from my mistakes and I went on. Your mother and I have been married for eighteen years now.

If you look at history, I hardly ever screw up twice at the same thing.

In these times, I read about children not much older than you who have actually killed themselves because of a bad grade, or a pregnancy, or any number of things they considered tragedies. Their choice was to give up. That's not the answer. Nothing is so wrong you can't recover from it.

One of the most important things is not to be so afraid of screwing up that you won't try something new. If you try and it doesn't go right, at least you'll know what doesn't work. From there you can make adjustments and get on another road, hopefully to a successful recovery. Sometimes it takes a few tries. But that's better than not trying at all. Then life would be boring and we wouldn't ever get anywhere.

Love,
Dad

"Divorce is a grown-up thing that shouldn't
have to hurt you, but it did."
MARTHA KASER

Martha Kaser

Martha Kaser is the kind of person who knows the names of every tree in the forest, scours the local newspaper front to back in any town she visits, and is a compulsive reader of museum exhibit signs and historical markers. She is also a lawyer who truly cares about her clients. Many of the cases that end up in Kaser's Albuquerque, New Mexico, office involve divorces, some relatively civilized, others laced with hatred and recrimination—power struggles between adults who insist on using their children as the battlefield. "I like it when I can work out a divorce without resorting to a lot of litigation," Kaser says, "when we can scream and cry and pound the table, but stay in the room."

Kaser's own divorce seven years ago was amicable. Her son, Matt, eight, likes having two birthday parties, and Kaser hopes that despite his parents' breakup he will not give up hope that marriages can last. After Kaser's brother divorced in 1983, she lost contact with his daughter, Lindsay, now twenty-two.

Dear Lindsay,

I think about you often, more often than I think of my other nieces and nephews whom I actually see. Anymore, you are made of vague memories and outdated reports from your grandmother, my mother. When I visit my parents in Michigan, I stare at the Margaret Atwood books and wonder about you. I read *The New York Times Book Review* and wonder who you are reading now. For the women of our family, what you read is shorthand for who you are.

My last memory of you is at your father's wedding to his present wife—sulking, pouting, reading pointedly during the wedding reception. For a bunch of educated people, our family is often dense about emotional matters. Some of us thought that day that you were spoiled and selfish. I did not understand then that for you, your father's remarriage was a day of loss, when your hope of resurrecting your family was finally ended.

Many families transmit information about painful topics through encoded, ship-to-shore transmissions, or by the game of triangulation. Information is transmitted from Person A to Person C via Person B ("Whatever you do, don't tell —— about ——"). These people are not bad people. They are just shy, sensitive and clumsy when it comes to affairs of the soul. Some families fear intense anger so much that they substitute stone-headed silence, sometimes for years rather than risk splattering pain everywhere. Two of our relatives did not speak for twenty years over the fallout of their mother's death. Then, not long ago, I saw them together, two old people sitting in the basement of a small church, in the middle of a lugubrious Protestant wedding reception, complete with Hawaiian Punch and pillowmints. They were trying to speak to each other. Sadly, they could not. The one was now stone-deaf and the other was not much better. They are trying, but it may be too late.

All this by way of apology, explanation, and exhortation. This letter is about divorce. You are an expert, having lived through your parents'. I am an expert in a different way: I have been divorced. Then I fell in love with a man whose divorce proved too painful for him to survive— he committed suicide six years ago. And as a lawyer, I have presided over several hundred divorces in the past six years.

So listen to your aunt, girlfriend. Let some of this penetrate your familial stubbornness. This is a prayer, and a hope, from me to you.

I recently came across a study which followed a large group of subjects over many decades. Children of divorced parents, the study found, died six years younger than children of intact families. They also smoked more, engaged in riskier behavior, divorced more often, and reported more stress. How can anyone be surprised? I immediately thought of lost children like you, and of several of my cases where the parties are busily grinding their children and each other into paste.

I tried to bring the study into a particularly horrible case where my client is a fifteen-year-old boy (I am supposed to tell the court what is "best" for him). His father, according to his mother, is a crook and a pervert. His mother, according to his father, is a greedy bitch. They responded to my recitation of the study's findings with five seconds of silence. Then Dad said, "I'm not fighting. She's the one who is fighting." Mom replied: "You know, he's been diagnosed as a sociopath."

Neither reaction acknowledged their son. This young man dealt with his parents' mutual hatred by demanding fifty–fifty timesharing. The first time I met him, he explained how he had divided a week. He told me how to calculate time down to minutes and seconds "so that you can be one hundred percent fair." "Fair to whom?" I asked. "Fair to everyone," he replied.

Inevitably, this tightrope snapped. He first rejected his father and would not see him except in court-ordered therapy. Then he refused to see his mother, after they had a particularly vicious disagreement over pot smoking. In the meantime, he got his driver's license—our society's only meaningful rite of passage. His father has promised him a new Pontiac Firebird or Camaro when he graduates from high school: He's staying with Dad. The parents continue to fight: crook, pervert, bitch, mercenary, sociopath, liar, liar, liar. Their son is lost.

One of the worst things that happens in many divorces is that reality is up for grabs. Children have difficulty knowing what to believe. Their experience before their parents' separation may be of a happy family, and the love of both parents. Afterwards, they must sort through the attacks of one parent against another. This campaign to discredit the other parent can be subtle and skilled, or akin to a psychological chain saw massacre—the result is the same. The child hears: "He never loved you [me]." "He's lied to us [me] for years." "She is a bad mother [wife]." "We [I] have been abandoned by him." "He is an alcoholic and a drug addict [as if I did not know this for years]."

Parents project their own anger onto the child's life with the other parent. I have had a five-year-old tell me, "My father tries to interfere with my court-ordered timesharing." How many times was this rehearsed with him before he came to see me? The child, meanwhile, loves both parents and may have a pretty good time with each one. Eventually, the discrepancy between what she sees and what Mom says about Dad becomes too painful to bear. It's akin to asking the child to hold two high-voltage wires—"Mom" and "Dad"—completing the current. To avoid electrocution, the child usually drops one wire completely.

In a divorce, who is right and who is wrong may matter very much to the adults involved, but it should not have to matter to the child. Kids want both of their parents. They do not want to be drafted into this fight. Unfortunately, once they are, they are good foot soldiers. Or, they have had to choose one parent over the other to save their lives.

My years as a divorce lawyer have made me realize how powerless children are. They own nothing except their toys, and even their toys can be the subject of a custody fight. I have had parents argue about where the stuffed animals should live, and where the Rollerblades should be. "I paid for them," says Dad. "But I'm the one who plays with her," says Mom. Neither parent understands that the child's toys are virtually the only thing she owns—and they belong with her, traveling from house to house when she does.

I have asked parents to try nesting, that is, leaving the child in the house and letting the parents move in and out. This suggestion is almost always met with disbelief and complete rejection. "How can you expect me to go from house to house and never have a place to live?" they ask. I ask, "How can we expect a child to do the same thing?" Yet we do, because we figure that they're just children and they don't have to go to work. I heard a young man report the results of traveling from house to house at a seminar on the effect of divorce on children. He said when his parents got divorced, his mom got this, his dad got that, and he got a suitcase. As soon as he turned eighteen, he said, he was going to pack his suitcase one last time and never be seen again by either of them.

I've wandered far afield in this letter. What I really wanted to do, Lindsay, was cry, "Come back to us, please. We miss you. We consider you part of us even though you are gone."

Good intentions cannot always overcome the effect of a long-standing fight, the sense of terrible injustice, the pain that has been visited, the choices you made in order to live in peace. In my work, I try to help figure out ways for people to divorce without hurting their children so much. I do it for the memory of my dead friend, for the memory of you, and because children deserve better than we're giving them. I say to you, Lindsay: I miss you and I love you, and I think of you in the world somewhere, a talented writer, I'm told, living your life, and trying to figure this out. Divorce is a grown-up thing that shouldn't have to hurt you, but it did. If you can ever forgive us enough, will you please come back?

Love,
Your Aunt Martha

"Don't Flunk Failure!"
BLAKE "SKIPPER" DUNCAN

Blake "Skipper" Duncan

When you work the land in West Texas, you learn a lot about hard labor, a lot about frustration and disappointment. But you also savor the smell of rain after a long dry spell, watch a newborn calf wobble to its feet, listen to the night songs of a thousand frogs. Skipper Duncan grew up in town, the son of a clothing merchant. But a visit to relatives in Nevada convinced him he wanted to be a rancher. His cousins wore big hats, chewed tobacco, and ran wild mustangs. "I wanted to be just like those guys," he says.

After decades of battling encroaching brush and struggling to feed his cattle on parched earth, Duncan, fifty-four, has distanced himself from his "addiction" to ranching. But he has more than a few lessons to pass on to his eighteen-year-old stepson, Randy.

Dear Randy:

You have skinned and boned-out hundreds of deer the last few years at our hunting camp, and now you are considering a career in meat processing. Soon you will leave home and go off to college to be entirely responsible for yourself. The success that will come your way in life will be great fun. It is the failures that will create the problems, but that's also where your most valuable lessons will be.

So far, as a student, the word *failure* probably makes you think of flunking in school. But as you get further into adulthood, the concept of failure will begin to include all kinds of new meanings. How a person decides to handle failure has a great deal to do with everything else in his life.

What kind of failure am I talking about? Remember my story about Hernández, who worked for me at the ranch long before I married your mom? I'd sent him to find a missing bull up in the West Lee pasture. He spent a whole day on horseback inspecting the cedar-choked canyons and dense mesquite flats, but to no avail. As he told me of his search, he spread his bandanna on the ground, using it as a map to show me his travels that day. Punctuating his Spanish with hand gestures, he convinced me that indeed he had looked on all sides of the pasture for the missing bull. The only side of the pasture he hadn't checked, he said, turning the handkerchief upside down, was the bottom side.

So did Hernández "fail" that day? Not in my book he didn't. He did his best and I don't count that as failure. Failure might come when you haven't tried all you know to try. Neglect can result in failure. But just plain bad luck isn't the same thing.

Sometimes, of course, what a person sets out to do is simply impossible. When you guide a deer hunter at our hunting camp, don't try to sneak up on a white-tailed buck from his upwind side. And don't expect to wean calves by simply driving them away from their mammas. These things don't illustrate failure; they illustrate foolishness. Wisdom is learning to recognize beforehand what ought to work. Wisdom is something you don't have a great deal of right now. But it will come if you are receptive to the lessons of experience.

Failure can be a great teacher but you don't have to fail personally in order to learn a good lesson. If Blake gets bucked off old Dunny because he failed to lead him off a few steps after saddling him and tightening the cinch, you might remember this trait is peculiar to most horses. And an unexpected bronc ride, unless your girlfriend is watching, is never to your advantage.

I read somewhere that Edison tried more than eighty different materials before he found what would eventually become the element in a lightbulb. Now that's persistence, and persistence works against failure, but doesn't always conquer it. Sooner or later we will all fail at something, so we have to learn to deal with defeat one way or another.

The kind of failure I want you to think about goes way beyond getting your nose a little bloody. We're talking shipwreck here. A hollow feeling will settle in the pit of your stomach and there will be a load on your shoulders that is more real than figurative. A sense of impending doom will stalk you day and night.

So how will you handle failure when it comes? There are three common approaches: dodge it, deny it or declare it. You probably can think of several ways people dodge a colossal failure. Alcohol and drugs are a couple of obvious escapes. They don't work.

Some people deny that the failure was their fault. Refusing to accept the consequences seems to be our national pastime. How many times do you hear something like this: "Really, Officer, I don't have an inspection sticker on my car because the mechanic can't get to me till next week." It's the mechanic's fault that the car wasn't brought in a month ago?

So when you fail, declare it. Lessons from failure begin when we step up to the lick log. "I screwed up, I failed" are difficult words to get out, but they are therapeutic—maybe even a wonder drug. My missionary friend, Terry Waller, says an admission of failure is like a confession: the first step toward forgiveness.

As you know, I'm now having to say, "I have failed in the cattle business"—a failure that will cost me part of my ranch. Hard words for a Texas rancher to say, believe me.

Will there be a lesson in my failure for you to take with you as you go off to college this fall? I think there is, and I think it has something to do with the spiritual side of life.

For the person without God in his life, failure can be devastating. But for a Christian, there is an option to handle failure quite effectively. And it's a good thing, because being a Christian doesn't mean that you won't take a licking every now and then. Sometimes that's the only way to learn a lesson He thinks we need to know.

Failure can even be a life-altering event, putting us onto another, better course. Our friend Dale Bates says that every time a door closed in his face, there was another door somewhere that opened. The harder God slammed the door, the more doors elsewhere were jarred open. I like that philosophy.

The prayer I start the day with is this:

> Please God, guide me and lead me and show me the way.
> Help me to make the right choices today.
> I know that it's true, when I pause to reflect
> That You won't get me in too much of a wreck.
> If it looks bad from here, You're standing on High.
> My trust is in You, Lord, till the day that I die.

So you see, Randy, successful people are successful because they learned how to handle their failures. You must learn to handle failure, too.

Make a sign for your mirror: DON'T FLUNK FAILURE.

Adíos and Peace,
Skipper

When A.C. Green's Los Angeles Lakers teammates heard that he planned to stay a virgin until after marriage, they were skeptical, to say the least. What about the lures of the professional athlete's lifestyle? What about the gorgeous women who hang out after games? "We give you six weeks," they told him. That was ten years ago, and they're still waiting for the six-foot-nine forward to lapse into temptation. "They sort of gave up on me," he says.

Self-restraint is just one of the ways Green, who in 1993 founded Athletes for Abstinence, tries to set an example for young people. At the A.C. Green Leadership Camp, inner-city kids have the opportunity to play basketball, but also to explore a variety of nonathletic career paths. "I'm trying to destroy the myth that you can only be successful through athletics," says Green, who now plays for the Phoenix Suns, a message he echoes in his 1994 book, Victory: The Principles of Championship Living *(Creation House). Ten-year-old Kevyn, Green's nephew, lives in Portland, Oregon.*

Dear Kevyn,

You kids laugh when you hear us adults talk about how tough it was when we were growing up. But you know what? I believe today doesn't even compare with yesterday. I shudder when I think of the gang activity so many of you guys growing up today see, and how inviting it can seem. Gangs give kids a false sense of belonging to a family, the illusion that they are with people who care about them and who will provide for them mentally and physically as well as emotionally. If you're in a gang, you feel powerful, like you have your own identity. It all sounds so good.

But to you and to my other nieces and nephews, as well as to my young fans across the country, I have this to say: Gangs and clubs— Skinheads, Crips, Bloods, whatever—don't provide a real image of what a family is or what a family is supposed to be. A family is not supposed to tear down and destroy, or divide things up like territorial animals. Rather, the objective of a family is to build up and support one another, and to repair the wounds of life.

"Just because you're a good athlete or a good performer
doesn't mean you're a good person."
A.C. GREEN

A.C. Green

Kevyn, one of the most important things I want to say to you is that I want you to be responsible. When you say you're going to do something, do it. Think about the result of the decision you're about to make. Don't run away from responsibility; embracing it will make you stronger and develop more character.

This brings me to the subject of sex. You're going to hear a lot about sex from school, from your peers, from TV programs and celebrities who will tell you when to become sexually active and how to be safe. But listen to your uncle: Abstinence is the only real form of safe sex. It's 100 percent guaranteed. Let's not see how close you can get to the fire without getting burned. Even if you've been sexually active before, you can still reclaim your virtue and pride by deciding to practice abstinence in the future.

I know it can be difficult at times. I know because I practice abstinence myself. It might not be popular or cool, but it's right for many reasons: You're obeying God by doing it; you're saving your body for someone you're committed to in marriage; you're developing greater respect for yourself and your body; and you're realizing that decisions that you make today have a direct effect on your tomorrow.

Restraint is not letting your emotions or your desires control you. If a young lady tries to pressure you into having sex, Kevyn, you should already have made up your mind that you're not going to do it before you even enter that situation. I hope you will pick your lady friends wisely, and not choose one who will put you on the spot. *But if you don't plan to succeed, you're planning to fail.*

We live in a society where many people hate being judged. I don't mind being judged. I want to set an example, to be someone who isn't afraid to have people look at my ideas, thoughts and options. Many of the heroes whose pictures you want to place on your wall—entertainers, athletes, politicians—fall down in other parts of their lives. They want your attention, but they don't want the responsibility of being a hero or the pressure that might come from that platform. I would like to muzzle half these so-called heroes because I know that you and thousands of other young people are excited by their talent. But just because you're a good athlete or a good performer doesn't mean you're a good person. I just wish these people could realize that they're making an impression on young minds, especially within the Green family. I hate seeing your generation substitute performance for character. Take a lesson from the story of David and Samuel in the Bible. God told Samuel that while man looks on the outside to judge, He looks into a man or a woman's heart.

Kevyn, I can't tell you how much fun it is to know you, how much fun it is to play basketball when I know you're out there watching with your brother and your cousins. I can count on you guys going crazy, giving "high-fives," throwing popcorn at people—just being yourselves. But I'm just as excited, Kevyn, by the thought of you growing up to be a responsible, reputable, God-fearing young man. I want to be the male role model you need, someone you can laugh with, talk to, cry in front of. I want you to know that you can count on me telling you the truth, even if you disagree with it, and I hope I can lead you to the greatest example of all, Jesus Christ.

In return, I hope you will take on the responsibility of setting an example for your little sister, Paris, and your little cousins. You are a product of a middle-class family, of a broken home, of a community doused with fear. But you know what, Kevyn? You can make it. You can make the difference in your family as well as in your community. I say to you, as I would say to any youngster in a similar environment: With the right attitude, education and family support, you'll succeed against all odds.

To all my nephews and nieces and kids everywhere, and especially to Kevyn Jermain Green, you are my heroes.

Love,
Uncle Jr.

Some children ask big questions early on: Why am I here? Where am I going with my life? Linda Kimble was like that, even at nine years old, walking a mile and a half to the United Methodist church by herself one Sunday when no one else wanted to go. In junior high, she began keeping a journal; in high school, she took up reading Tolstoy and Dostoyevsky; in college, she visited a different church every Sunday, trying to find one that fit. "I was looking for something to base my life around," she says. "It wasn't a search for meaning. It was a search for the one true church that would follow the teachings of Jesus Christ as found in the New Testament."

What Kimble finally found was the Church of Jesus Christ of Latter-Day Saints. Her decision to become a Mormon triggered conflict within her family and created a rift with her best friend that is only now healing. But she has never regretted it. "It was a struggle for me to be strong enough to be baptized, regardless of what my friends and family thought," she says. Twelve years ago, Kimble and her husband, Steve, a dentist, built a brick house in Arthur, West Virginia, looking out on the Alleghenys. Kierstin, eleven, is the youngest of their six children.

Dearest Kierstin:

Kieri, you may wonder why I used your "grown-up" name to start this letter. This is a grown-up subject, and one that is very important to me. And since you just turned eleven, the time is right to share things that you are old enough to understand and not forget.

Of all the wonderful qualities that make you special, the one your father and I have noticed more than others is your determination and commitment to reach your goals. We watched as you struggled as a little girl to learn to skate, pulling yourself up, regardless of bruised knees and scratched elbows, to try one more time to make it around our bumpy concrete patio.

That same determination served you well as you learned to balance yourself on the bike, learning quickly because of your great desire. Many times you were left to learn something for yourself, because the

"Even if I do achieve success, some of those I love
may never notice it. But I will know
and God will know."
LINDA KIMBLE

Linda Kimble with daughter Kierstin

rest of us were off doing things which seemed, at the time, more important. That infuriated you, but made you all the more determined to do it, and do it well.

You've already seen the challenges that commitment sometimes brings. That is why it is so important that we know deep in our heart that what we are committed to is right, because we may have to suffer the tauntings of our friends or our family as a result of our choices.

When I made the decision after almost two years of study and prayer to join the church, I made it with a realization that those I loved might not understand. Already, I had been cast off by my closest high school friend and college roommate, due to a misunderstanding about religion and a mutual friend. We had discussed religion many times, and she and a group of our old friends had met with me and tried, unsuccessfully, to stop my continuing interest in the church. They did this because they loved me and felt what I was doing was not for my good. But even though others may have what they feel is your best interests at heart, you alone must choose what you feel to be right. It was a difficult choice.

I'll never forget the awful, lonely feelings I had on my eighteenth birthday, when I returned from each class to find more of her belongings moved out of the dorm room, without explanation and without warning. We have since been briefly reunited, and have forgiven each other, but the old closeness is gone.

This label of being "different," Kieri, is one you may find difficult. I've seen how young people seem to long to be a part of the crowd, in clothing styles, language, activities. But in this increasingly confusing world, there is a big difference between choosing to wear a popular basketball player's jersey because everyone else has one and choosing a religion because it is more accepted by the world.

Our church has high standards that are often hard to meet. Jeff, Valori, Jimi, and Dani, with sleepy eyes but determined spirits, rose an hour earlier every day during high school to attend an early-morning scripture class at the chapel. Their friends didn't understand, but you see how much stronger their love of the scriptures has become.

You were just a year old when I began teaching those scripture classes to the high school students. Every year since, you have gathered with us early each morning for family prayer before I left for class. It was not easy for me to turn the responsibility over to Daddy for getting the smaller children off to the school bus in time. But he and I agreed that nurturing the spiritual life of our children was every bit as important as caring for their physical needs.

That kind of commitment started from the day we became husband and wife. The choice your father and I made to be married in the temple meant that we had to travel across country, because there were no temples on the East Coast at that time. As I sat in the warm August sun, looking across the rolling hills of my West Virginia home, preparing to leave, I felt the weight of that decision to be married far away from family and friends. But I did not doubt that it would bring me more joy than sorrow. When Jeff was born, one month after I had received my university diploma, there was no question as to where I felt I should be: in the home as a mother! Daddy still had several years of dental school to finish, but we felt that if we carefully managed the money he received from the GI bill, and his summer work as a housepainter, we could give our children the wonderful gift of having a full-time Mommy!

It was not always easy. I remember one particular day when I felt despair at the thought of years of doing mountains of laundry, rinsing out endless dirty diapers, washing a revolving stack of dirty dishes in the kitchen sink, and chasing dust monkeys under the children's beds! I renewed my commitment with the thought that if I were working outside the home, I would most likely be working for people that I didn't even know, whereas I had the privilege of spending my life working for the ones I loved best. Immediately, my job became easier. Sometimes, I even smiled and nostalgically kissed the socks or dresses before putting them away in the loved one's closet. No one knew but me, but I was remembering for whom my work was done, and so reminding myself of my great love for each of you!

As the only one in your school class who attends our church, you perhaps already have felt a longing to be more accepted by the others. We all felt that loneliness last December, when some of my family did not approve of Jeff's wedding in the temple. But the appreciation of others does not always come.

One bleak night I sat on Gina's bed, so tired I could barely move, and felt unappreciated for the hard work of the day. I leaned upon the windowsill and gazed out at the starlit sky, through the yard, and down toward the meadow. My thoughts somehow turned to the wildflowers blooming along the path through the woods and meadow. Then I thought that there probably was at least one beautiful flower, perfectly formed in color and symmetry, that no one had ever noticed. But that didn't matter because its Creator had seen and noticed and appreciated!

With that inspiration coming to me in the still quiet of the night, I came to better understand that no matter how hard I try in my imperfect way, and even if I do achieve success, some of those I love may never notice or acknowledge it. But that shouldn't discourage or distract me from the goals I seek because I will know and God will know. And that is what matters most of all.

I am so proud of you, Kieri! I want you to remember that you have within you the power to overcome all odds, all the challenges you may face, as long as you know for yourself what is right and you make that decision based on study, prayer, and faith.

Love You Forever,
Mommy

"You don't lose your identity by loving
someone else—you enlarge it."
STEVE ROBERTS

"Dear Children, we can call your name.
You are people of principle."
COKIE ROBERTS

Cokie and Steve Roberts

Steve Roberts asked for Cokie's hand in the garden behind her family's stately old home in Bethesda. Her father, Democratic representative Hale Boggs of Louisiana, was watering the tomatoes at the time. "You know, sir, your daughter and I want to get married," Roberts began. "I know you have some concerns about the religious differences. We will have some problems, but I think we can deal with them." The congressman replied, "You're right. I do think you'll have some problems, but not half as many as I would have if I tried to tell Cokie whom to marry."

Almost thirty years after exchanging wedding vows in that same garden, the Robertses—Cokie is a news analyst for ABC and NPR; Steve is a syndicated columnist—say that the joys and rewards of their "mixed marriage" far outweigh the difficulties of joining two religions. "I just don't think we human beings are very different from one another," says Cokie. Steve now tends the garden his father-in-law began: In 1977, the Robertses bought the Bethesda house from Cokie's mother. Friends and family gather there often—for Christmas and Passover, birthdays and Sundays—continuing the long-standing family tradition. The couple co-author a nationally syndicated newspaper column. Their daughter, Rebecca, is twenty-five; their son, Lee, is twenty-seven.

Dear Lee and Becca,

The hardest thing I've ever done was tell my parents I was marrying your mother. That might seem odd to you. After all, Grandpa and Nana have given us nothing but love and support during our twenty-nine years of marriage. But you have to understand the history.

Both of my parents were children of immigrants. They were not formally religious, but they grew up surrounded by Jews, and to this day, almost all of their close friends are Jewish. So you can imagine how troubling it was when their wayward son went off to college and started dating a Catholic. They openly admitted their fears: that they would feel awkward in our house, that their grandchildren would somehow be "strangers." Even as Mom and I got more serious about each other, my parents' disapproval continued to shadow our relationship. For a long time, we assumed we had no future.

It took a lot of late night phone calls, a lot of long walks around the lake at Wellesley, a lot of tension and a lot of tears. But gradually I began to discover something I never thought possible. My parents were wrong. They had let their fears blind them. They had focused on what divided your mother and me—labels, theology, clergymen—not on what united us.

In the years I'd been away from home, I had come to see things differently. Religious labels were not important. Mom and I were more alike than different. We shared a core belief in a moral code that we wanted to live by, and to pass on to our children. In fact, I realized, many of the virtues I most admired in Mom—her charity, her compassion, her concern for others—came directly from the nuns who had taught her. How could I resent her religion if it had helped create the person I loved?

I was very young then, barely twenty-three, and very scared. I was the good child, always wanting to please my parents, not defy them. And at times, words choked in my throat. Mom and I had an understanding that I would ask her to marry me during a romantic carriage ride around Central Park. The ride was practically over—and my bride-to-be was pretty irritated—before I managed to speak the magic words.

Then Mom insisted that I come to Washington and formally ask her father's permission before we got engaged. But before that, she added, I had to tell my parents what I was doing. I waited until the last possible second. My plane was about to take off. I called home and got my mother. "How are you?" she asked. "I'm fine," I croaked. "In fact, I'm going to Washington and Cokie and I are getting engaged." She burst into tears. I hung up.

Gradually, things got easier. To my parents' credit, they were willing to learn and to change. As my father once put it, "It would be a lot easier to oppose this match if it weren't so obvious that she's the perfect girl for you." And Mom's parents made an enormous effort to make my family feel comfortable. We got married at home, not in a church. We had a *chuppah*, a traditional Jewish wedding canopy, and I broke a glass, another ancient Jewish ritual. Arthur Goldberg, then ambassador to the

United Nations and an old friend of Mom's family, said a few Hebrew prayers. I've always thought of that ceremony as a good metaphor for a happy marriage. When in doubt, be flexible. Make everybody feel included and respected.

I was still learning about myself, however, learning what I could do and what I couldn't. I agreed to be married by a priest, Mom's Uncle Robbie, because it didn't matter to me who signed the marriage certificate. But I balked when the church asked me to sign a promise that I would raise our children Catholic. I'll promise *you* anything, I told Mom, but that's all. We don't need any more outsiders telling us what to do. Mom agreed, and the church relented.

What we did promise each other was that our children would be raised in both traditions, and we've tried to keep our word. It gives me great pleasure when my parents come to our house every year for a Passover seder. But I also know that things can get pretty confusing— for all of us. When Lee wanted to go to Georgetown Prep, a Jesuit school, I had to battle through my own prejudices once again and remember what I had told my parents: Forget labels, focus on reality. Prep turned out to be the perfect place. The Jesuits, Lee, were just what you needed, and you understood that before I did.

Then there was the trip to Israel. You were eight and six at the time, and we took a children's Bible along, visiting sites sacred to both of our religions and the places where my grandfather, Abe Rogow, had worked as a young Zionist pioneer early in the century. I wrote a piece about the journey for *The New York Times* and concluded with an account of a night we spent in Jerusalem. While walking to dinner we were trading riddles, and Lee said he had one. "What," he asked, "does a Catholic and a Jew make?" When we were stumped, he gave the answer: "Me."

I was stunned by the reaction to the newspaper article. Many Jewish readers were outraged: because I had married a non-Jew, because I had taken my "hybrid" children to the Holy Land, even because I had criticized the food. The most offensive letters suggested that my sainted Zionist forebear must be spinning in his grave over his grandson's betrayal of the faith.

The writers didn't know, of course, that at the end of his life, when he barely recognized anybody, my grandfather always asked for your mother—his Catholic granddaughter-in-law—because she had been so kind to him. Even now, I seethe at the memory of those letters, at the pigheaded prejudice they reflected. But I did, accidentally, get a chance to respond. A year or two after the trip to Israel, I was standing outside a shopping center in northern New Jersey, watching a Republican congresswoman greet her constituents during a congressional recess. When I was introduced to one voter she recognized my name and said: "You're the one who wrote that article about Israel! I bet, now that you're older, you realize you were wrong."

My response, to say the least, was impolite. My long-simmering fury boiled over. "I can't believe how prejudiced you are," I shouted. "And the older I get, the more I realize that I made the right decision. I married the right woman."

I still feel that way. I still believe that you can stay true to yourself while embracing a different tradition. I still believe that you don't lose your identity by loving someone else—you enlarge it. And I still believe that you should not let others impose their prejudices on you. Not even your parents.

Love,
Dad

Dear Becca and Lee,

"How do you do it?" and "What do the kids think?" Those are the two questions we've been asked repeatedly over the years. To the first, I've always just laughed and joked about doing a lot of shopping and cooking around the holidays. (That has the advantage of truth, but doesn't come close to doing justice to the frantic domestic scenes when I'm preparing for thirty-five for Chanukah on December 22 and forty-five for Christmas three days later, trying to keep the red and green decorations discreetly stashed in a drawer until the blue and white ones come down.) To the second question, I used to give a glib answer, like, "Are you kidding? They get two sets of presents, they love it." By the time you were five or six years old, the answer was more complicated than that. Now that you are adults, I understand, mostly because you've told me, just how complicated it really is.

Clearly, it would have been easier for you if we had raised you in only one faith, or even in none. Still, our extended families helped us celebrate both traditions. When we got married, my sister's Irish Catholic mother-in-law gave us a mezuzah for our doorpost, and later sent off her family's christening gown at the appropriate times. My mother has presented us with menorahs, and your Roberts grandparents have often stayed in town after our seder to celebrate Easter at my brother's. Even so, you've pointed out that we raised you the way we did because it worked for us, not necessarily because it was best for you. It's one thing, you've said, for us to each bring a distinct religious identity into this mix, another for you to be expected somehow to meld them.

But if we had not found a way to be inclusive, rather than exclusive, about our beliefs, there would have been no you. Daddy writes of the shadow over our relationship when we assumed we had no future. I read those words and am somewhat surprised to feel tears springing up. Not because I'm reliving the fears of those long-ago days, but because it fills me with sadness to think that we might have missed out on the life of love and friendship we have been so blessed to share.

After we had been married for ten years or so, I remember thinking, "I must have been crazy, to think that I might have let religious labels get in the way of this love." That's the classic reaction of young people who have gone away from home, separated themselves from their roots. But now that I am older, I've learned that this love would not be what it is had we abandoned our faiths and not tried to pass them on to you. It's not just that we would have been hurting our families—although that's terribly important to both of us, as you know. It's that we would have been hurting ourselves and each other and ultimately, you.

For each of us, our religion is a defining part of who we are. It informs us with a set of principles, as distinct from prejudices, a compass providing a sense of direction in an evolving world. For one or both of us to have put those principles aside in the name of simplicity would have meant putting aside a fundamental part of who we are. And in all our married years together, not one of the arguments which typically spice married life has been about religion.

But what does that do for you? What direction do you take when your path has been so much muddier than the solid concrete of my many years in Catholic schools, or Daddy's membership in Jewish youth groups? What, in the end, are you? What is the grown-up answer to Lee's little-boy riddle: "What does a Catholic and a Jew make?"

Dear Lee and Becca, I have no fear for you. I know who you are, even if you don't yet. You might not easily be able to define yourselves as Catholic, or Jewish, or both. But you are knowledgeable about and interested in both traditions and we have confidence that you will carry them on. Daddy and I now know you as adults. We've watched Becca care for my sister as she was dying, Lee rise early in the morning to drive for the city's soup kitchens. We've rejoiced in the way you readily assume responsibility for yourselves and for others, the way you defend your beliefs, the way you live your lives. We have seen you praying at High Holy Days and at Sunday Mass, lighting candles on the Chanukah menorah and on the Advent wreath. Dear Children, we can call your name. You are people of principle.

> With love and admiration,
> Mamma

Tom Laney, a St. Paul, Minnesota, autoworker and former president of the United Auto Workers Local 879, has been called a dreamer, a radical, a relic, even a Communist. But if he dreams, says Laney, his reveries are simple ones: a world where all human beings are treated fairly, where decent, dignified work is available to all who want it. Idealism is in his blood, the legacy of his father, a country doctor, of his mother, a devout Catholic who taught him always to fight for the underdog, of his heroes: Martin Luther King, Jr., and Victor and Sophie Reuther, early organizers of the UAW.

Laney's father, now eighty-nine, instilled another passion in his son: football. The family makes a yearly pilgrimage to Madison, Wisconsin, for a Badgers game, and the importance of such outings has come home to Laney now that he is a grandfather himself. "All of a sudden my kids were grown," he says, "and the things we should have been doing as a family didn't get done because I was away or working long hours." Given a fresh chance with his one-year old granddaughter and namesake, Laney, he has no intention of missing the opportunity again.

Dear Laney:

You have meant quite a change in my life, and in your grandmother's too. For one thing, we were wondering if we would ever become grandparents. For another, you've reminded me how much I wish I'd been more of a comfort to your mother that time she flipped over her bicycle, or to your Aunt Carmel when she cut her nose sledding. I wish I had hugged my kids more, spent more time with them, done a better job of sticking up for them when they were being treated unfairly. So you mean another chance for me.

I like that sign over your crib: "God danced the day you were born." Your arrival helped pull us through a difficult time. While your mom was delivering you, we were trying to understand why your eight-year-old cousin, Sarah, was dying. Why do kids have to get cancer? It just wasn't fair.

"No one ever taught me how hard it can be
to stand up for what is fair."
TOM LANEY

Tom Laney with granddaughter Laney Henehan

Sarah was able to hang on until your mom could take you to meet her on your second day, making a connection that will be with you always. Thinking about Sarah always makes me wonder about fairness. What is fair? Why are so many children without parents like Sarah's—your Uncle Peter and Aunt Terese? How can we make life fair for everyone? These are big questions, whose answers are, I think, in us all.

The first thing to know about fairness is we all have trouble with unfairness, especially me. Feel free to consult me anytime about my many mistakes. I think I can save you some time.

When I was eighteen, a cocky, spit-and-polished paratrooper home on leave, I repeated some things at the dinner table I had heard about African Americans in my all-white platoon. My dad, with uncharacteristic patience, responded by telling the story of how he began his career as a family doctor in Chicago's poorest neighborhood. He told us how he came to love the people there who, though they had practically nothing, somehow managed to stay happy and care about each other. He told how, when he delivered babies, people were always interested in where he was going and whether the baby was a boy or a girl, and how he was always invited to the celebrations. This was an African-American neighborhood, where the goodwill continues to impress your great-grandfather at age eighty-nine.

In a very careful way, my father taught me that to be fair, I had to know people before I formed opinions about them, and that hatred is always based on ignorance. This was an important lesson, and opened the door to learning about civil rights, affirmative action, and the necessity of good, family-supporting work for everyone.

My mother drilled us, too, reminding us of world hunger until we joked about leaving the broccoli on our plates, which really upset her— she was very serious. Years later, when she could no longer recognize me, she was still carrying a copy of *Time* with Nelson Mandela on its cover.

The most dangerous people you will meet will be those who recognize unfairness but tell you nothing can be done about it. Don't waste much time with them. And never tolerate leaders in power positions who argue against fair action.

It might seem strange that I would write you a letter about trade unionism when you are still so small. But the labor movement is where

I've spent a good chunk of my life, and where I've met many of the most idealistic and important people I've known, most of them assembly line workers.

It seems like just a few moments ago that your mother was crunching along an Austin snowbank on a frigid Minnesota day, union banner in hand, facing off Army troops to support striking meatpackers from Local P-9. It was Martin Luther King, Jr.'s birthday, and the governor of Minnesota, the son of a steelworkers' union organizer, had called out the troops against the strikers. It was not very fair.

Days earlier, your Aunt Carmel was having a heated discussion with the police as she walked a picket line, doing her best to persuade them that they were on the wrong side. Both your mom and Carmel were helping the meatpackers in their fight for fair wages and work. These are my favorite images: Our kids on picket lines, in marches and demonstrations, always taking sides with the underdogs. When we got home that night, your grandmother was incensed that scabs were on television talking about stealing the strikers' jobs, because the pickets were so peaceful.

There is no place like a picket line to learn about what is fair. Don't ever cross picket lines. Just go right up to them and talk to the strikers, and you'll learn more about fairness and economics than they can teach you in school. You'll also meet some of the best people you'll ever meet in your life and make some good friends.

A couple of my favorite boat rockers are Vern Gagner and Mose Thomas, guys I've worked with for over twenty years. They and some other "radicals" on the assembly line taught me volumes about solidarity, honesty, tenacity, courage, persistence and friendship—the key ingredients of fairness. Assembly lines can be very unfair places. We deal constantly with work speed-ups, firings, huge numbers of work injuries, favoritism, inequality and discrimination—all sorts of troubles.

Workers like Vern and Mose have always taken the side of anyone treated unfairly. Sometimes their stands meant they were called names: "Communists," "radicals," or "plant closers." But I can't remember either of them ever looking the other way or finding a convenient way to avoid controversy.

Guys like this make for a very hopeful world. Most are overworked and underpaid, but they always seem to be cheerful, bright and compassionate, whether they work on farms, in factories or in offices. It was people like this who formed my union more than fifty years ago, who in the 1960s sat in the front of the bus and at lunch counters from Montgomery to Greensboro fighting for civil rights, who sat down in factories and marched in Washington and Birmingham.

As I write this letter, forty million in our country live in poverty, most of them children. I wonder how such unfairness is allowed in the world's richest country. As I'm thinking about this, a coworker hands me a flyer about how easy it is to draw welfare payments in our state. I asked him how is it fair that someone like him who makes well over twenty dollars an hour makes fun of poor people? It's not fair that workers who hoard overtime scapegoat the poor and then complain that their kids can't find decent jobs.

Fairness is about balancing opportunity. All of us hear about fairness when we are growing up: Don't pick on other kids, stand up to the bullies, share stuff, don't take advantage of other kids. Change always starts with us, just regular people talking about solutions. Just regular people telling the racist and the bully that we don't want to hear a racist joke, we don't want to see someone else abused and bullied. That is a lot to do. It is also surprisingly hard, so sometimes we just pretend we didn't hear the joke, or didn't see the bully. I was taught about fairness in school and church and home. But no one ever taught me how hard it can be to stand up for what is fair. In my own life, I've had vast stretches of time when I've battled alcoholism. I was gone a lot, a traveling drinker, stopping for a drink in St. Paul, another one in Madison, another in Chicago. Your grandmother taught me a lot about fairness just by refusing to give up on me. She really pulled the family through. And because there were so many years that I was unfair to my family and friends, I have to try to be extra fair for the rest of my life to make up for this.

The Reverend Martin Luther King, Jr., said we all have a responsibility to dream. He meant that we have an obligation to ourselves and to others to think about what would make an ideal family, neighborhood and world. He said we shouldn't take shortcuts for reasons of comfort or convenience. We shouldn't settle things just to get them out of the way. He also tried to act on his dreams. He talked about his fears, but he also kept finding the courage to go back into the struggle time after time, even when he knew he might be killed.

Fairness isn't automatic. It needs to be organized and oftentimes fought for. Sometimes fairness is confused with justice. I think justice is a more mechanical, formal and legal kind of idea than fairness. We might wait for others to give us justice. Fairness is more gutsy. It is about the way we live our lives, from the playground to the factory floor. Kids have a wonderful sense of fairness: It's the adults who create the racism, greed and competitiveness that injure so many children. So we'll be needing your help on this.

I look forward to reading Martin's "Letter from a Birmingham Jail" with you.

Give your friends and all of us lots of hugs. Grow flowers. Most important, fight for your dreams.

Love,
Grandpa

"He is no fool who gives what he cannot keep to gain what he cannot lose," the missionary Jim Elliot wrote. They are words that Ken Trautmann tries to live by, a principle he uses to guide decisions, like putting aside his dreams of becoming an Olympic cross-country runner in order to dedicate his life to serving Jesus Christ. "I decided that if I was going to live my life for something you could be sure of, maybe running wasn't for me," he says.

In Cedar Falls, Iowa, Trautmann and his wife, Lynn, home-school their children, Katelin, eight, Rebekah, nine, Christy, eleven, and Seth, two. Says Lynn: "We want to teach them character and self-discipline, things we think we can teach better at home." Instruction in history, reading, science, and spelling is her responsibility; Ken, who teaches elementary school in nearby Waterloo, takes over math and computers when he comes home from work. "I want them to see that their relationship with God is more important than anything," he says. "There won't be a U-Haul following the hearse— you don't take things with you."

Dear Christy, Rebekah, Katie, and Seth:

I want you all to know that your biggest or your most highly visible achievements are not the most important ones. Such feats may be the things that people remember you for or congratulate you about, but your real success comes from all the hard work, pain, trial, failure, joy, broken dreams, and commitment it took to achieve those few moments. In other words, self-discipline. The achievements that will build success in your life are the ones people never see, the long hours when everyone else is in bed, the early mornings when others are too tired to get up. It's the dedication to your word, even when it hurts to fulfill it. It's doing what you've committed to do even when others don't understand, going on when others have quit, continuing when others mock and criticize. It's not making excuses. It's going it alone when necessary. It's doing it silently and with humility. It's living without complaining. This is success.

"I've had to learn that suffering and sorrow are helps,
not hindrances, in my life."
KEN TRAUTMANN

Ken and Lynn Trautmann with children Christy, Katelin, and Rebekah

I have no great achievements that people will talk about. I have no great accomplishments for which I will be remembered. But that's okay. Those things would soon be forgotten, and if they were all I had, I would be empty. But what I do have is the self-discipline to continue to reach toward my goals and desires, regardless of the praise and notice of others. To accept the circumstances of life as opportunities for further growth. To know that I have achieved when others do not see it.

What I have learned I'd like to share with you, not out of a sense of great accomplishment, but rather out of a sense of small successes and victories that help me deal with whatever problems or tasks I have before me. This is what I would want for you: A life of small but consistent disciplines that will build your character and lead to success. I've had to learn to adjust my goals. When I was in high school, I wanted so much to play football. But as a child, I fell down while ice-skating and received a severe concussion, and the doctors felt playing football would be too risky, so instead I focused on running track. When I went to college, I had to finish a four-year degree in six years, because I changed my major many times to find what was right, finally settling on teaching.

I've had to learn to go on my own when others would have taken the easy route. During cross-country practice, when others might have relaxed, I kept working, rising early in the morning for some quiet time even though it would have been easier to keep on sleeping. I've had to learn that suffering and sorrow are helps, not hindrances, in my life. I've had to learn that the praise of others is not to be sought above the approval of God, that standing alone is to be prized above belonging. I've had to learn to have confidence in doing what God has called me to do, regardless of the results or the acceptance of others, to accept the circumstances of life without complaint, viewing them as opportunities for growth.

You know that we do things differently than many other people, but part of me hopes that you haven't even registered the difference (though I know from some of our conversations that you have). Most people don't home-school. They don't go without a TV. Many families have mothers who work. Many families have more than one car. We want you to accept as "normal" things that we believe will build self-discipline in your lives, and not only that, but also come to love and embrace them. Many times as I was growing up, I thought how difficult some of the things were that I had to do, and that many of my friends didn't have to do. But I can see the fruit of those experiences, and I'm thankful for the self-discipline that I gained. I trust that you will accept these things in your life too, and allow them to form the necessary attitudes, character, and discipline for success.

I love you all,
Dad
1 Corinthians 9:2–27

Park on Main Street in Kouts, Indiana, stroll down the sidewalk, order a doughnut and a seventy-five-cent cup of coffee at the Coffee Cup, and you are likely to run into Ralph Levy, or others like him: ordinary, hardworking folk who go to church on Sunday, stay married for more than half a century, buy a new Oldsmobile every other year (and pay for it with cash), and head to Florida for a few weeks each winter, just to warm up.

Sixty-two years ago, Levy got his first job at Fuller Brush, knocking on doors and making his pitch, opening his case to show off the dust mops and clothes brushes and brooms—polite, neatly dressed, eager to be of help. "I never thought I would be a salesman," Levy says. "I didn't have an education, so I thought I'd never be successful. But being a salesman has been an opportunity to be of service. The customer doesn't have to go to the store. If I don't know the answer to a question, I can call the main office. She doesn't have to wonder about it. I get an answer. I give a personal touch." An old-fashioned way of thinking, but one Levy would like to pass on to his grandchildren, like Joel, nineteen, a premed student at Purdue University.

Dear Joel:

I would like to relate to you some of the obstacles I had to deal with when I was your age. I was a shy boy, raised on a farm with two sisters and seven brothers. We wore hand-me-down clothes and walked a mile to a one-room schoolhouse every day. My parents took us to Sunday school, and we always put God first in our lives. I left high school after my second year because things were hard on the farm, and my dad needed my help to make ends meet. It was the Depression and he couldn't afford to hire a farmhand. We didn't have a tractor, so we plowed fields with four horses.

At the age of twenty-one, I was on my own to find whatever job I could. I worked for $1.00 per day my first summer. I had $10.00 in my pocket, and no car, when my older brother, who was successful with the Fuller Brush Company, talked to me about becoming a Fuller Brush

"Meet customers with a smile and never argue with them:
You may win the argument but lose the sale."
RALPH LEVY

Ralph Levy and grandson Joel

dealer, selling housecleaning supplies door to door. This was in September 1933, when the country was still in distress from the Depression. I decided to try it, so my dad let me use his Model A Ford for six weeks. But he told me that I wouldn't make any money and would wear out the car.

So never get discouraged, Joel. I had no experience in meeting the public, but I was determined that if my brother could do it, so could I. In just one month, I bought my own car, a 1928 Chevy, and paid $100 cash for it. After a year, I bought a brand-new two-door Ford and paid cash for that, too. And two years later, I moved up from being a dealer to the position of field manager.

Since you have just graduated from high school and are going to Purdue University this fall to study in the medical field, you will need to have the determination to reach your goal.

In the sixty-two years I have been with the Fuller Brush Company, I have seen many changes. World War II caused a big adjustment in my life. I went from making $600 a month as a manager for Fuller Brush to $21 a month in the Army, which was quite a letdown. But dealing with change has taught me to be satisfied in whatever situation I found myself. When I was promoted to branch manager, I had to compete against managers with college degrees. Even though I never finished high school, in five years the branch I took over went from last in sales for the district to third or fourth out of fifteen.

Another big adjustment occurred when I retired from management in 1972 and became a dealer part-time. Although I am now eighty-four years old, selling has helped to keep me mentally and physically fit, in addition to providing income.

As a manager, I prayed for direction when making decisions, which made it easier to make the right decision. Always put God first in your life and let Him show you the way. Joel, I know that you have a strong faith in God. Don't ever lose that.

Another important trait to have is honesty. There have been many times that I could have taken advantage of people or of the company, but I didn't. A few times, the company shipped more products than I had paid for, but I always called them to correct it. I am always honest with my customers and tell them to the best of my knowledge what a product will and will not do. Then when I call on them again, they trust me and will buy on just my word. You will never be sorry for being honest.

I have learned that to make a good impression on customers, you must be neat appearing, with shoes shined and a necktie when wearing a coat. You must meet customers with a smile and never argue with them: You may win the argument but lose the sale. Once, when I was calling on a house, a woman opened the upstairs window and asked who was there. I told her that I was the Fuller Brush man and I had a free gift for her. She said just a minute and then dropped a string from the window and told me to tie the gift on the string. I tied it on, told her thank you, and left.

When a customer has a complaint, I make an adjustment by replacing the item, or exchanging it for any other item of equal value. One customer called to say that her hairbrush was defective. She said the handle was still good, but the bristles were worn out. I asked her how long she had owned it, and she told me ten years. In spite of the fact that this was just normal wear, I replaced it for her, anyway.

In summary, life has its ups and downs, but if you will set goals and then work hard, even through adversity, you will do well. It will take self-discipline and determination, but goals that are worth achieving do not come easy. Always treat others with respect and honesty. In the years I have worked for Fuller Brush, I have always treated my customers, employees, and superiors that way. Most important, if you put your trust in God, and strive to live your life for Him, all other things will be added unto you. May God Bless you in the future and help you to meet all challenges.

In Love,
Grampa

Not long after Margarethe Cammermeyer was expelled from the National Guard for stating that she was a lesbian during a security clearance hearing, a burly, tough old Marine approached her as she was walking in to work. "Do you know what the most important thing to an infantryman is?" he asked her. Cammermeyer said she didn't. "The most important thing to an infantryman is his buddy," the Marine said. "And you can be my buddy and share my foxhole anytime." Then he put his arms around her, and they both wept.

Following her dismissal, Cammermeyer stood firm and eventually won her case in court. She lives quietly in Seattle, Washington, with her partner, Diane Divelbess, and continues her work as a nurse specialist at the American Lake Veterans Administration Medical Center. Cammermeyer was born in Norway, and grew up on tales of World War II Resistance fighters. Their courage and determination encouraged her to remain resolute in her own struggle. Perhaps her grandchildren, Makayli and Jake, will draw similar inspiration from their grandmother's story.

My Dearest Grandchildren:

For days I've been pondering what I would write in this letter. What do I most want you to know and understand to make growing up easier? I thought about the virtue of honesty, of how important it is to be honest with yourself so that you can be honest with others. But you may have already heard how honesty resulted in my leaving my marriage and then costing me my military career. That is true, of course, but there really is more I would like for you to know.

As I was growing up, I was naive. I thought my options in life were only those that I heard about on radio, saw on television or experienced at home. I thought the only option women had was to have children. I did not plan to get married. My goal was to be the first woman general in the Army. But when your grandfather, Harvey, asked me to marry him, I thought that was what I was supposed to do. I did not think I had other options and I could not think of a reason not to marry.

"Be true to yourself. But with honesty
comes the responsibility to accept the consequences."
COLONEL MARGARETHE CAMMERMEYER

Margarethe Cammermeyer

We had a busy and good life as we created our family. We built our dream house on eight acres; we were living completely self-sufficiently. But sometimes our dreams are not reality. Although I deeply loved my children I was so unhappy; at times I was dangerously close to suicide. And I finally realized that I had to leave the marriage. I felt such confusion, sadness and guilt. Even now I weep thinking about it, and when I look at the picture of my sons from that time, I am astounded that I could have left. But I had to.

After leaving, I entered the world without a name, without family, home, money or security. It was very frightening and lonely, but it was what I needed to do for myself.

The next few years were ones of figuring out who I was. I learned that I was a competent, whole person, a good nurse, military officer and mother. At the same time, I felt very alone and my life was emotionally empty. I also recognized that I was not interested in a new relationship with a man, but I was unsure what that meant.

Then I met Diane. There was a comfort in our relationship, with love, caring and trust. There was an emotional connectedness which I had not experienced before. I knew then who I was and why I had needed to leave my marriage.

When I was questioned about it later during a military security clearance and I replied, "I am a lesbian," I shocked myself as much as the investigator. Because although I felt a tremendous sense of relief, there was suddenly the uncertainty of what impact this was going to have on my military career. Since I believed that being honest was the most important attribute one could have as a person and as an officer, I thought surely the military believed the same. But they didn't.

So where is all this leading? Well, with honesty comes the responsibility to accept the consequences. That is the time when your personal convictions and moral courage will be tested.

When I was growing up, my parents told me how they worked with the Resistance fighters during the Nazi occupation of Norway. I remember wondering if I would have had their courage. Would I have the moral courage to fight for what I believed was right?

When the military decided I would be discharged because of my statement that I was a lesbian, I decided it was time for me to take a stand. Being honest should not mean losing a career. It was very intimidating, challenging the United States government. I was afraid of losing the relationship I had with my sons, with my friends, co-workers and clients. I feared the rejection I had been taught that people could expect upon divulging that they were homosexual.

Despite my feeling of vulnerability, for the first time in my life, I felt a true sense of purpose. I felt that there was a higher power working through me. I was supposed to be here on earth, now, and this was my job.

I soon realized that my military career would be over, regardless of what happened to my case. However, I would not resign my commission. The policy to deny people the opportunity to serve in the military because of their sexual orientation is wrong, and I believe it is unconstitutional. I decided that if I were to be discarded and rejected by the military, at least I would put up the best fight I knew how.

We subsequently won our case in court, when the judge ruled that an individual could not be discharged from the military because of the prejudice of others. This decision was vindication for the thousands who had been discharged before me, whose voices had not been heard.

My return to the military became anticlimactic for me, because I learned so much along the way about what is really important in life. I learned that being honest with myself, about myself, made me a whole person. I also learned that we are more than just ourselves. It is through each of our efforts, fighting for good, standing up for justice, that our lives become full, good and bountiful. Finally, I learned that no matter how much I give, I always receive so much more in return in love, support and encouragement from others.

So, my dearest grandchildren, I would only wish for you the happiness of knowing, believing and being true to yourselves. Being honest with yourself truly frees you to express the glorious spirit that is within you. Being honest and true to yourself will give you the courage to take on all the challenges that life may offer, and which you can never imagine. You will succeed and your life will be full of love as you love.

From Your Bestemor

The wager probably seemed to Uncle Louie an opportunity to teach his grand-nephew the perils of making stupid bets. But to Bill Damon, then a twelve-year-old growing up in Brockton, Massachusetts, without a father, what happened said a lot about his grand-uncle, about the man's integrity, his sense of adventure, his larger-than-life presence in Damon's life. It was the top of the ninth inning, and Ted Williams was at the plate. After Williams had hit two home runs, Damon bet the older man $1 that the left-fielder would hit a third in his last at-bat for the Red Sox. "I'll bet you a hundred dollars to your one that Williams can't do it," Uncle Louie replied. He was wrong, of course. And the next morning, true to his word, he took the boy to Brockton Savings Bank and opened an account in his name for $100—an amount that "seemed like all the money in the world," recalls Damon, director of the Center for the Study of Human Development at Brown University, and author of Greater Expectations (Free Press, 1995).

Forty years later, Uncle Louie remains a powerful figure in Damon's life, someone he admires and wonders about, and whose memory he wants to pass on to his children, including his youngest, Caroline, twelve.

Dear Caroline:

I'm sure that to you your twelve years feel like forever, but for me they have sped by like an express train, rushing past some local stops I would have liked for us to visit together. Your life has been crammed with school, summer camp, friends, family, and all the ups and downs of growing up. You and I have had many talks. Yet through all the commotion and conversation, some things have slipped by. One is that I have never told you anything about my Uncle Louis— "Louie," as we all knew him. He was actually my grand-uncle, and your great-grand-uncle. Louie did not live to meet you or your older brother and sister, although he was the source of your brother's middle name.

"Youth should be a time of high hope, early accomplishment, bold leaps of faith—and, yes, wholesome ambition."
WILLIAM DAMON

William Damon and daughter Caroline

In his prime, Louie was one of those men you see in almost any picture of American city streets prior to 1950, wearing dress hats, coats and ties, and polished leather shoes.

Louie was born in New York City around the turn of the century, the son of immigrants from a German-speaking part of Europe. One of the few things Louie had from his father was a drinking mug with a German inscription which Louie would translate with a kind of rueful pleasure. "We get too soon old and too late smart."

Louie's childhood lay obscured in the apocryphal tales self-made people often tell to their families. I know that he grew up in the midst of hardship and financial need. I'm less sure about his claims that he never knew cookies were supposed to be round, since all that his mother could afford were the baker's broken leftovers.

Louie made his way up from poverty in the freewheeling 1920s. Did he really insure bootleggers during the days when buying liquor was prohibited? (The insurance part was legal, he would take pains to emphasize.)

The only sure thing that I have from his youth is a daguerreotype metal plate with young Louie's photograph molded on it. He is standing in front of a battered slumscape door, wearing a baseball uniform and assuming a pitcher's stance. One special element of the picture does shine through the obscurities of the distant past, a quality both timeless and very American—the determination in the young boy's eyes. Call it will, or call it ambition. It was the central ingredient in Uncle Louie's story as well as that of millions of others who forged a future for themselves in this country.

Nowadays, *ambition* is not a fashionable word in many parts of our society. The whole notion of "getting ahead" is considered crass, overly competitive, somehow unnatural. I think that something has been lost. Wholesome ambition is a natural part of youth.

When the Great Depression hit, Louie was the only one in the family with any money. I should tell you what he did with it. With no children of his own, Louie became a benefactor to the children of his brothers and sisters. He never made it through high school himself, but he sent five nieces and nephews to the best colleges they could find. Nor did Louie stop with that generation. When my own father joined the Army during World War II and then failed to come back, Louie was still there, providing for me just as he had for my uncles and aunts, my mother and my older cousins.

Generosity needs to be its own reward in life, because it is always met with a certain amount of skepticism and thanklessness. Soon after I dedicated one of my books to Louie's memory, I got a call from someone Louie had helped through college. How, he wanted to know, could I harbor such fond memories of that son-of-a-bitch? The caller was a fine person of sterling character; there clearly was some truth there. In fact, Louie was not popular with everyone. He was gruff and direct; he had little patience and spoke with a take-no-prisoners frankness. I was too young to bear the brunt of his temper, but I did see it in action on two or three terrifying occasions. I have heard a litany of his misdeeds from others in the family. But I also remember that, when Louie died, people came from everywhere for the funeral. It was over twenty-five years ago, and that was the last event that brought the family together as a whole.

I could tell you more about the things Louie did for me, but I would rather tell you about something he refused to do for me. I was in sixth grade and fancied myself a baseball player. I had been playing the game long enough to have acquired a permanent role: first baseman. The only competition for the spot on the school team that year was a kid so inexperienced he did not know enough to straddle the base before the other infielder threw him the ball. To this day, I remember how he would get his feet all tangled up. But sadly for me, the coach was this kid's homeroom teacher. In one of the most momentous injustices in the history of the human race, this inept boy was chosen to start ahead of me.

I said nothing around school. One day, though, Louie noticed me moping. I poured out my complaint to him, and he asked me what I was going to do about it. I gave him a blank stare. He said, "Go talk to the coach. Tell him the facts." In my twelve-year-old mind, the thought of doing this felt as impossible to me as jumping off the Empire State Building. I stared blankly at Louie a bit longer, then blurted out: "Maybe you can give the guy a call? He'll listen to you." With the same kind of rueful smile that he used when translating the saying on his German mug, Louie told me, and I still remember his exact words, "Naw, you're apt to speak up better for yourself on a thing like this."

I wish I could say that this story had a happy ending, that I convinced the coach to let me play and drove in the winning run for the league championship. The fact is, I still kept my mouth shut and sat out the season in misery. Still, the lesson somehow sank in. I did learn to make my own case vigorously whenever I felt I was in the right. I learned another lesson too: Don't be too quick to do for others what they are able to do for themselves. Although this rule certainly has its limits, I believe it is a wise caution for parents who may care so much about their children that they rob them of the chance to build their own strengths. I first learned this lesson from Louie. I would hope that you have learned it from me.

Uncle Louie grew up in a world very different from the one I grew up in, and you are growing up in a world that is far different still. You have not had the economic hardships that troubled Louie's youth, nor have you lived with the same fears—polio, the Bomb—that intruded on mine.

Yet your generation faces its own hazards. Some of these may, in fact, be aggravated by the absence of an outside threat to mobilize against. I have seen too many young people drifting through their lives without a sense of purpose, without anything to believe in beyond their own immediate self-gratification. They are wasting a precious chance to build the skills and values they will need to face the future. Youth should be a time of high hope, early accomplishment, bold leaps of faith—and, yes, wholesome ambition. When I look into the eyes of young Louie in that photograph, I worry that we are creating a society where timidity and cynicism have replaced the adventurous sense of purpose young people traditionally have thrived upon.

Louie died in 1969. If you visit his grave, you will see that the gravestone lists, at his request, his rank as an enlisted man in the U.S. Navy, where he served during World War I. I think about him often. I wonder what the Navy meant to him at age eighteen, and why he reached back fifty years for the inscription on his tomb. Louie accomplished many brave, generous, and colorful things in his lifetime. Was there an act of heroism on the seas that overshadowed them all? Did he remember the Navy as the place that gave him his start as a young man breaking away from a limited past?

I shall never know the answers to these questions. I can't even answer similar wonderings about my own course in life, nor about yours, though I am hoping to learn more as time goes on. Such learning is slow and uncertain, but it keeps us going. Although we always grow too late smart, the excitement is in the trying.

Love,
Dad

Cedric Clute's hand-built house in Volcano, California, has fifty-five windows, mementos from his days as manager of Earthquake McGoon's, a popular San Francisco nightclub where luminaries like Woody Allen and Walter Cronkite rubbed elbows with the common folk under the beneficent eye of jazz musician Turk Murphy. But in 1975, Clute and his wife, Jan, decided to chuck the late nights, gridlocked traffic, and frenetic pace of city life for a quieter existence.

Retired now from his job as curator of the Amador County Museum, Clute, sixty-five, spends his days writing, taping his radio show on local history, dipping into the couple's 10,000-volume library, and filling the woodbox with winter fuel. (Two years ago, the Clutes finally traded in kerosene lamps for electric lights.) As a "flatlander" new to country life, Clute learned about trust, hard work, and getting to know the people you deal with—values he'd like to pass on to his grandchildren, Deirdre, four, and Davis, one.

Dear Deirdre and Davis:

I'm writing this letter knowing it will be a few years before either of you can read it, but I know your Mom or Dad will read it to you. Later, I hope, both of you will read it for yourselves. I want to tell you how your Nana and I came to live up here in what you kids like to call the "Big Park," how we came to build our house, and why we love living in the country.

Fifteen years ago, Nana and I moved 150 miles from San Francisco to the Sierra Nevada. We felt that life in San Francisco was too frantic and that there should be more in life than just trying to make money. With a $2,000 down payment, we bought seven acres of land east of Sacramento, near the town of Volcano. We rented a little cabin on Sutter Creek for $100 a month, and Nana's brother Don and a couple of his friends came down from Washington State to help us build our house.

One of the first things Nana and I learned to do up here was to look people in the eye and deal with them as equals. In the city, we usually dealt equally only with people just like us, and mistrusted or were indif-

"Try to move through life a little bit slower,
with a little more thought."
CEDRIC CLUTE

Cedric Clute with grandchildren Davis and Deirdre

ferent to others. I don't know if this was our fault; everything moved so fast we just didn't think about those things. But all this changed when we started to build our house.

For example, there was Doug at the hardware store in Jackson. A shake of the hand, and we had credit and were able to buy supplies. There was A. J. Harris, who put a gas-powered pump in our water well and told us to pay him when we could. And there was eighty-year-old Sidney, an African American who had come out west to Mokelumne Hill with some gangsters from Chicago. That was in the 1930s, but we met Sidney in the 1980s, sitting in his yard in an overstuffed easy chair, hand-cutting roof shingles from a big round of sugar pine. His dog, Boy, an old Doberman, was running around the yard with a chicken in his mouth. We bought ten bundles of shingles on credit, but not before sealing the deal with a round of whiskey at Sidney's kitchen table.

Another man, Tom, was as hardworking a guy as I've ever seen. He put in the floor of our house, but it wasn't just any floor: It was called a rammed-earth floor, and Tom mixed cement, dirt and water together, and pushed it in a wheelbarrow up a hill and into our house. I think it took about 100 loads to cover the concrete base. Then, before it hardened, Tom put on these crazy shoes with big metal grids on the bottoms and stamped all over the floor. When it was finished, it looked as if we'd laid down a floor of expensive tile!

Nana and I learned something important from each of these people. We learned the importance of trust when we were dealing with Doug at the hardware store in Jackson and when Jim Harris put in our well pump. Tom Lambie taught us something about hard work and discipline, and Sidney Trice made Nana and me think about courage when he told us about being the first black man in Calaveras County.

Both of us worked very hard to repay the trust these people placed in us, and sometimes we had to take jobs we didn't like. Nana washed a million dishes at the St. George Hotel, and I pulled weeds and bartended, but it was necessary if we were to pay our bills. We made new friends, met new people, and took advantage of each new opportunity. Today, Nana is the children's librarian at the Amador County Library, and is very happy. Last year, I retired from my job as curator of the county museum, and I'm learning to become a house-husband. Both of us enjoy our work.

You know what else we've learned? We've learned to work with our hands as well as our minds, and now we can cut lumber, hammer nails, put in windows and lay shingles in the right direction—we've learned to build a house! Both of you can learn these things, too. Try to move through life a little bit slower, with a little more thought. Take the time to look at people, really look at them, and you'll learn just as we did.

Both of you will be starting school soon, and it will be tough, don't ever forget that. The problems of guns and gangs and overcrowding won't go away by the time you begin the first grade. But you can't let that stop you.

A hundred years ago, here in the Mother Lode, lots of children didn't even get to go to school. Some boys had to go to work, and the only place they could get work was in the gold mines. There were two jobs these eight-, nine- or ten-year-old kids could do: One was chopping wood ten hours a day to keep the fires going in the room where they processed the gold ore. The other was to be a "bucketeer," working 3,000 feet underground where the temperature was over 100 degrees.

After the crew dynamited some rock, the bucketeers' job was to scramble through the rubble and dust and pick up samples of the ore, then put them into a leather bucket slung around their necks, head for the surface in an elevator called a "skip," and take the ore to the assay office. Then, just as quickly as they could, they'd head back down for more of the same. The bucketeers were breathing quartz dust all the time, and their lungs were chewed up pretty bad. They were lucky to make it to twenty. But they did get paid: twenty-five cents a day, seven days a week.

Today, Deirdre and Davis, you both have choices that children born in 1895 didn't have. You can become an astronaut, a magician, an engineer, an ironworker or a fireman. Or you might decide to become an astronomer, a musician, a poet or an artist of some kind.

I'd like your Nana and me to be around forever. We'd be able to watch both of you grow up and marry and have children and grandchildren of your own. But I know that isn't possible. We'll be gone, but our letters will be with you. I hope every once in a while you'll re-read them and remember that Poppa and Nana have loved you from the moment you were born and will love you forever.

I'll end this now, but not before wishing that you both will love life, laugh at life, and live life to the fullest!

Your loving Poppa

"When your integrity slips, even for one seemingly small
moment, there can be lifelong consequences."
MAJOR DAN FLYNN

Dan Flynn with children Billy and Tricia

Dan Flynn joined the police department almost by accident, taking the entry exam in Dade County, Florida, on a whim one day rather than twiddling his thumbs outside while a friend finished the test. Then the results came back: His friend failed. Flynn passed. He had considered law enforcement as a profession before: Both his uncle and brother-in-law were police officers. And Florida didn't seem like a bad place to spend the winter compared with New York, where he was going to community college and working in construction. So he gave it a shot.

That was twenty-three years ago. In his work, says Flynn, now in charge of the Metro Dade Police Department's Professional Compliance Bureau, which includes Internal Affairs, "I constantly need to remind myself that I see people at their worst." He has to work, he says, to remember that his perspective is extreme, and to resist the urge to overprotect his children. But his kids have other things on their minds: Billy, twelve, wants to join the Air Force; and Tricia, ten, talks of becoming a church missionary.

Dear Billy and Tricia:

I know to you it must seem like a very long time since I was a teenager, but to me it doesn't seem long at all. I clearly remember what it was like, and I remember a lot of good things: my first date, school parties, football games, my first car. On the other hand, I also remember a great deal of internal conflict, awkwardness and occasional insecurity.

What I remember most are the moods I experienced, and the new attitudes I acquired. My father died when I was fourteen, and I remember feeling isolated and unable to communicate with my mother. She seemed old-fashioned and self-righteous, and unable to understand many things I was going through.

I usually listened to adult advice, but when I wanted to buy a motorcycle, my mother objected and we argued. I felt that, when it came to motorcycles, I knew better than she. A motorcycle, I said, would be economical and wouldn't take up much space to park. Besides, several of my friends had them. My mother countered that it was easy to fall off motorcycles and that there was little protection in an accident. I badgered my mother until she grudgingly relented.

Soon after I got the bike, a Suzuki X6-Hustler, I took a pretty girl named Gina for a ride, feeling on top of the world. We were whizzing along at sixty miles an hour on a busy New York highway, when we rounded a bend and saw a car stopped across our lane, headed the wrong way. I couldn't cut to the right because of moving traffic, or to the left, because of a high curb. We hit the car broadside. I slammed against the side of it. Gina flew over my head and over the car. As she fell, the bones in her right ankle shattered like glass, and she was in terrible pain as we waited for the ambulance. My own injuries were less severe, although I was bleeding and I couldn't walk.

I needed crutches for six months after that, but my injuries eventually healed. Gina, however, still walks with a heavy limp more than twenty-five years later. I was devastated with guilt for what I had done to her.

A few years after the accident, I moved to Florida and became a police officer, and my perspectives about safety and responsibility changed sharply as I saw firsthand the carnage that occurs when young people feel they are invulnerable. One Sunday about 3:00 A.M., I was assigned to investigate a traffic accident. A car was reportedly submerged in a canal, and I raced to the scene with my red lights on and siren blasting.

When I arrived, I found a smoking, badly damaged vehicle in the roadway with a man on the ground next to it in a pool of blood. Some passersby had stopped, and as soon as I got out of my squad car, I could sense the shock in the air. On the bank of a canal which ran along the road lay a sixteen-year-old boy whose name, I later learned, was Jimmy. In the light cast by the road flares I was setting out, I could see he was bleeding from the head. Another boy, fifteen, was lying on the damp ground moaning, even more severely injured. A third boy was dead, trapped in the car they were riding in, now upside down and completely submerged in the canal.

Later, at the hospital, I learned that Jimmy was a straight "A" student. He had an after-school job and was serious about going to college and building a future. Normally, he showed good common sense and was, by all accounts, a good kid. But he had a restricted driver's license, which meant he could drive only during the daylight hours and was not allowed to use his father's car without permission. On this particular Saturday night, his father was out of town, and his friends persuaded him to sneak the car out. After driving around for a while, they stopped and bought some beer with false identification that one boy produced. When the accident happened, Jimmy had been speeding and swerving all over the road. His actions caused the death of one of his friends and serious injuries to himself, another friend and an innocent motorist.

Jimmy was charged and convicted of vehicular homicide and multiple traffic violations. His driving privileges were revoked indefinitely. He had to pay a large fine and was on probation for several years. When all the lawsuits against him and his family were concluded, he and his parents were left in debt for the rest of their lives. But perhaps the worst outcome of the accident, aside from the death that occurred, was the psychological mark it left on Jimmy: His guilt was devastating. He became withdrawn, deeply depressed, and would need years of psychological counseling.

Although my motorcycle accident was not as serious as Jimmy's, there were many similarities. It was a powerful learning experience for me to be personally involved in a serious accident as a teenager, then to see a similar situation through the eyes of a police officer a few years later. As a teenager, I viewed my accident as a mistake—a bad thing that happened to me. As a police officer, I viewed Jimmy's accident as the terrible consequence of a good kid deviating from his normal way of doing the right things.

Now, when I look back, I realize that the key to both situations was integrity. In general terms, integrity means having a set of positive values and putting them into practice. People who have integrity are the same both in public and private. They don't have one way of behaving around some groups of people, like parents or teachers, and another way around friends. And when your integrity slips, even for one seemingly small moment, there can be lifelong consequences.

In my years of law enforcement, I have known people with great integrity, and others with little or no integrity. People with no integrity always seem to have a better life in the short run. If they're involved in criminal activity, they sometimes have a lot of money. They drive fancy cars, have great houses and boats, and hot relationships. The problem is that life in the fast lane never lasts too long. They may have an exciting time for five years, or if they are lucky, ten. But then they end up in places like jail or drug rehabilitation—or in the morgue. Meanwhile, people who have integrity and stick to what they know is right avoid these traps. This is not to say that they never have problems, just that they tend to avoid serious problems of their own doing and are better equipped to deal with problems in a rational way.

When I was a teenager, one of the last things I wanted was a lesson in values or integrity. I felt I knew a lot, and that I'd learned what I needed to know about values in Boy Scouts and in church. In this regard, both of you are pretty mature and have demonstrated good values. Integrity, however, is an advanced notion, one you often learn only from painful mistakes. Thus, at the cost of sounding preachy, I desperately want to guide you away from the kinds of irreversible mistakes that Jimmy and I made.

If you don't have the courage to stick to what you know is right, you could wind up being the first of your friends to become an adult very suddenly. You could be the first unwed parent, the first drug addict, the first prisoner or AIDS patient. It is far easier than you think to meet any of these fates, and I can tell you that they are not reserved for any particular ethnic group, income level or social status. All unwed parents, drug addicts and prisoners were once little boys and girls who knew the difference between right and wrong. Their problems began with their early choices, choices that could have turned them in another direction had they a sense of integrity.

In closing, I want to pass on to you a basic strategy I use in determining if a choice I am about to make is within my personal boundaries of integrity. I ask myself three simple questions: Is it legal? Is it balanced (is my decision fair to everyone concerned)? And how will I feel about myself if I do it? If my answer to any one of these questions is negative, I know I'd better rethink my decision. From the bottom of my heart, I hope you will use this or a similar strategy for making your important choices.

Love,
Your Dad

Passages

"Luck plays a central role in all
successful lives."
DR. ESTELLE RAMEY

*Estelle Ramey with son Jim and (left to right) granddaughters
Caitlin, Meg, and Sarah*

A young student once asked Dr. Estelle Ramey if she didn't find it tiresome being married to the same man for forty years. "Not nearly as tiresome as getting used to some other man's foibles," she replied. Ramey, professor emeritus of physiology and biophysics at Georgetown University Medical Center, has never been shy about speaking her mind: "I was one of those lucky babies born outgoing and not afraid of most things," she says. Now that she's almost eighty, there's even less reason to keep silent. "When I was younger, I had to mind my manners," says Ramey. "But I'm secure in my position, and nobody has anything out there that I want. I don't really care what people think."

One subject the scientist is always happy to talk about is women, and how they differ physiologically from men—a topic that has been the focus of much of her research. And she delights in pointing out the advantages of not having a Y chromosome, such as greater longevity and increased resistance to stress. "We're a remarkable sex," she says, "and we've never been given the credit or the ability to change the world that we might have." Ramey lives in Bethesda, Maryland, with her husband, James. The couple have two grown children and four grandchildren.

To my children and grandchildren:

As I approach my eighth decade, my thoughts begin to assume a dynastic quality. You are, after all, my passports to immortality. In turn, you are hostage to the genetic code of your parents and their parents and their parents in turn, back to the Garden of Eden.

You have been molded irrevocably by our beliefs and prejudices and hopes and fears. All parents want their offspring to be exemplars of virtue and achievement and happiness. But most of all, we want desperately for you to be safe—safe from disease and violence and self-destruction. If we could, we would shield you from all the minefields of the world we helped to create. But we can't. I can tell you about the joy of reaching the mountaintop but you will have to do the slogging to get up there.

It has always been a brutal world. I was born during the First World War—the bloodiest in history up till that time. That was quickly upstaged by the Great Depression, by Hitler's atrocities and the even bloodier Second World War. These are the events which shaped my youth. Infectious disease was the leading cause of death and there were no antibiotics, no chemotherapy, no elegant surgical and visualization techniques. My peer life expectancy at birth was forty-nine years. My life expectancy today is eighty-five, and rising. You will live even longer, and the health care costs will continue to rise and rise. The gods say: "Take what you want and pay for it."

Before I was ten, I had survived diphtheria, scarlet fever, whooping cough, and a variety of other potentially fatal infectious diseases. Many of my contemporaries didn't make it. I know now that fate had given me an invaluable gift—I was born lucky. Luck plays a central role in all successful lives. A towering genius or a Moses born today in Bosnia or Somalia or in one of the other hellholes of the world would be born to "blush unseen and waste its sweetness on the desert air."

All of you were wisely born in America to parents who value you above rubies and have the wherewithal to give you all the skills and education you can absorb. Your greatest gifts, however, are not your good brains (and good looks) but your family heritage of decency, and our hatred of bigotry and meanness and intolerance. You have all given evidence of knowing that no man or woman is an island. It is the joy of my aging heart to see each of you develop—in the word of an ancient people—a "mensch." Freely translated, that means a decent human being with a great capacity for love.

I did not have your economic security as a young girl. My mother was widowed during the Depression and left with three young children. I was the eldest and the only girl. My mother was an immigrant with no education or saleable skills. Her own vulnerability made her fiercely determined that her daughter would not go naked into a cold world. From my earliest years, she urged me to get all the education there was. My mother wouldn't have known what the word *feminist* meant, but she knew that women, like men, needed to develop strong legs to remain standing in life's hurricanes. And education was the key.

Most immigrant families felt this way about their sons but thought a "good" marriage was the only security for a daughter. My mother wanted her daughter to develop her own tools of survival. To be independent. To be Somebody. She never doubted I could learn anything, however difficult. And because of her faith in me, I never doubted it either. I have tried to impart that same confidence to my children and grandchildren—girls and boys alike. You don't need a Y chromosome to be an achiever.

Against all odds, I became a research endocrinologist, a medical school professor, and ultimately a national lecturer on the effect of sex hormones on longevity and human ability. Aside from my mother, my career was fostered entirely by men that I worked with. Men stood at the entrance to every door to advancement, and again, my luck was in evidence. I had the great good fortune to work with men who, when asked "Which is more intelligent, man or woman?" always answered "Which man and which woman?" There have always been men like that—just not enough of them.

Early on, I met an extraordinary man for his time (or for any time) who, like my mother, believed that women as well as men should have a crack at that ancient Greek definition of Happiness: The Achievement of Excellence. He has been my support and life's companion for fifty-four years now, and was very helpful in producing all of you.

At this stage in my life, I don't do much agonizing about mistakes I may have made. It is not the stupid things I did that disturb my sleep. It's the things I didn't do: the words I never spoke, the little kindnesses I omitted because I had my eyes on a goal and I was running so fast to get there. These are my deepest regrets.

The most painful memories I have are of my mother's pain because she couldn't buy me that special dress for the prom, because I had to work at menial jobs after school, because I had to wear unfashionable castoffs from my "rich aunt." I never told her how unimportant all those things were to me compared to the priceless gifts she had given me of unwavering love and confidence. I thought she knew.

And by the time I learned the need for words, there were no longer ears to hear. She was dead. I learned too late that words can be weapons or they can be life enhancing. I have in my life received honors and honorary degrees, and each time I stand up there to receive the accolades, I feel my mother is beside me, saying, "See, I told you to get an education." And I say, at last, "Thank you for everything you gave me."

If I could leave you with any advice, it would be to speak words of caring not only to those closest to you, but to all the hungry ears you encounter on your journey through a cold world. Stop on that mountain climb to bring along those less agile or well endowed. It will make the view even more beautiful when you get to the top.

For my own epitaph, I ask that it be: "I loved and was loved and all the rest was background music."

Your lucky forebear,
Estelle Ramey

A good psychotherapist, psychologist Richard Cutler believes, "has to be absolutely rooted in reality. You have to face it, and to be able to judge when other people can face it." Cutler's own roots took hold in the tiny crossroads town of Nottawa, Michigan, where his father farmed and ran the general store. His parents, Cutler says, taught him perseverance, generosity, and compassion—as well as old-fashioned common sense. But growing up in a close-knit, rural community taught him other things, as well. "There was an egalitarian atmosphere," he says. "I learned that in a fundamental sense, nobody is better than anybody else, and self-esteem is based not only on self-respect, but on how much you contribute."

In 1987, Cutler closed his practice, shifting his energies to writing and consulting, with time out for a weekly round of golf. After a heart attack last year, he dropped fifty pounds, changed his diet, and gained "a much deeper appreciation of being alive and being fortunate." In Ann Arbor, where he lives with Polly, his wife of forty-seven years, he spends as much time as he can with his family. Rebecca, his oldest grand-daughter, is fifteen.

Dear Rebecca,

When I was fifteen, my life was unbelievably different than yours. We were poor. So was nearly everyone we knew. Between working the land and running my dad's general store, we managed to keep body and soul together. But we had no electricity, inside plumbing or central heating. Few families had cars.

We farmed with horses, and nearly everything involved heavy physical work. The harder we worked, the better off we were. We bathed twice a week—need it or not—sitting in a big round galvanized tub, but we washed our feet every night to keep them in good shape. Bad feet meant less ability to work, and serious consequences.

By your standards, my life then was pretty primitive, but there were admirable aspects as well, and this is the context for the rest of what I write. True, we have gained in many ways in this last half century, but

"Trust is vital to our lives, and crucial
to our dealings with others."
RICHARD CUTLER

Richard Cutler and granddaughter Rebecca

we should make sure not to lose the values and attitudes that shaped my generation.

Many people back then had no money. I recall someone often coming into our general store to get a handful of crackers and a ten-cent ring of bologna, destined to be the family's supper. "Bill," they would say, "I'm a little short right now. Can you trust me for this?" The answer was almost always, "Sure. We'll charge it until times get better." The exceptions applied to people who could work, but didn't. These few were viewed as lazy, or no good, or in some other way not worthy of trust. But even they didn't starve, because they would go to the Wednesday night pot-luck supper at church, where no one was refused free food, and could take home what they wanted.

This taught me an important lesson. Trust is vital to our lives, and crucial to our dealings with others. Without it, relationships become unreliable, and our personal lives become chaotic. Gaining trust is easy: Treat others with regard and respect, present yourself with taste and dignity, tell the truth, be honorable and ethical. Above all, be constant and predictable, so that others feel secure about what to expect from you. And having gained a person's trust, never betray it.

In my one-room country school, to which we walked each morning, we began to learn to read and write the very first day. By the end of first grade (actually the second year), everybody was expected to read, and everybody did. People who failed the expected standards didn't pass and had to repeat the year, without disgrace, so long as they tried and didn't misbehave. We earned approval based on how hard we worked, how quickly we grasped things, and what we offered to the general good of the community. Here I learned that self-esteem is based not only on what you are but on what you contribute. This may seem harsh, but in a nowhere-near-perfect world, judgments about contribution and productivity are made all the time.

Most country work was hard, but there were some pleasurable exceptions, which I recommend to you. One of these was digging potatoes. A really prize hill might have five, six, or, wonderfully, even seven good-sized spuds, plus numerous others the size of aggie-marbles, which could be wiped off and eaten, with no concern for a little soil left on them.

I learned something from potatoes. There were rules about how to cut them up so they could be planted: nothing smaller than half a potato, with no fewer than three eye-sprouts. I figured that two sprouts and a third of a potato would do just as well—by using the same number of potatoes, I could plant more hills and, incidentally, do less work. But this was a short-lived enterprise. My dad caught me, and asked, "What the hell do you think you're doing?" When I told him I was saving on seed potatoes, he said, "Everything needs food to grow. To give those potatoes a good start in life, they need plenty of nourishment, and enough sprouts to make sure that at least a couple will come up. If you do it your way, you won't get enough good hills to matter, and the seed potatoes will be wasted." He added later that it was the same with anything you invested in, whether it was money, your mind, or your whole life. So, Rebecca, please don't short yourself on your investments.

One of the most important lessons I learned, growing up as I did, was about sex. Sex is a very powerful desire in our lives, but sex isn't love. We were taught very early that sex involves responsibilities. If an unmarried woman became pregnant, the man whose child she carried married her, sometimes literally at the point of a shotgun. And marriage was viewed as a permanent relationship, so that it was folly to run the risk of having to marry somebody whom you didn't love just for the sake of sex.

If it is only a physical act of pleasure, sex becomes exploitative, shallow and trivial. When love, sex and marriage exist together, they give us transcendent joy, happiness and ecstasy. But love takes months or years of patience, sharing, maturity and understanding to grow.

Rebecca, what awesome blessings you enjoy! A loving, intact family, a fine education, a generally secure environment, a country which is free and which offers great opportunities.

Your greatest blessing is not material comfort, though, but freedom. In this country we can make choices and decide most things for ourselves. This great freedom implies equally great responsibility: to choose wisely not only what is right for us, but also for others and for the general good of humanity. My dad put it very well, and very directly, as was his way: "We may be poor, but by God, nobody can tell us what we have to do."

You know I am seldom as serious as this letter sounds, so I will close on a lighter note: Life is meant to be fun, and fun is a sure antidote to disappointment. A million things have brought me joy, or laughter, or most important, the experience of beauty. Read. Plant a potato, and discover a treasure chest of new ones when you dig them. Walk down a northern path in springtime, and try to count the dogwood blossoms and the trilliums. Read Shakespeare. Discover love. Then look up at the stars and reach for them.

Love from your Grandpa

"There is a quality, a soul of youth,
that doesn't have much to do with how old you are."
DAVID OLDFIELD

David Oldfield with sons Ben (left) and Jeremy

In many tribal societies, becoming an adult is marked by a series of rituals and tests. But America offers young people no formal rites of passage, no guidance in leaving youth behind. And too often, says David Oldfield—whose workshop manual, "The Journey: A Creative Approach to the Necessary Crises of Adolescence," is used in school systems, churches, and youth organizations across the country—teenagers create their own initiations to fill the void, becoming mothers at fourteen, joining gangs, carrying guns, or trying in other misguided ways to find meaning, power, self-knowledge, and belonging.

Oldfield's own search for meaning took him to Yale Divinity School and eventually to Washington, D.C., where he founded the Center for Creative Imagination in 1980. "Imagination always takes you to the edge of possibility," he says. "In my work, the questions I'm always forced to ask are: What next? Why not? What have we forgotten? What are we afraid to try?" When he's not giving talks or leading seminars, Oldfield can be found at home with his wife, Merilee Janssen, and his sons, Ben, ten, and Jeremy, thirteen.

Dear Jeremy and Ben,

What if we've been wrong?

What if "growing up" isn't what life's about after all? What if this whole mad rush toward adulthood is an illusion, a scam, an enchantment from which we desperately need to awaken? What if Jesus was being literal when he said, "Unless you become as children, you will never enter the kingdom of heaven"? The planet has been in the hands of grown-ups for some time now, and we're about as far away from heaven as you can get. So maybe it's time to haul out the white flag and surrender, to admit we don't know how to give you what you need most to live in this world. Maybe it's time this whole "role model" business was put in reverse, and we learned from you instead.

Even the term, "grown-up," seems strange: It suggests that a time comes when you're supposed to stop growing. When I was your age, I thought my dad knew exactly who he was, what he wanted from life and what life wanted from him. And he may have, knowing him and the times he lived in. But you don't have a dad like that. I thought by now I was supposed to have my answers to the big questions, answers that would stay pretty much intact until I died. But it hasn't been like that for me: the identity crisis that started when I was your age just keeps rolling along, changing color, shape and texture now and then, but never disappearing. I never knew what it took to be a man instead of a boy, or if there was something I was supposed to feel, or think, or prove to make me different.

The first time I truly felt myself to be a man—my own person—was when I was divorced from my first wife, and that strikes me as a very sad statement. What I've read about how other cultures initiated their young into adulthood makes me yearn to live in another time, another place. To be a father was one of the scariest adventures of my life, and once again, there was no map or manual to tell me how to do it. But to think of yourself as "grown-up"—that is, done growing—denies the natural cycle of change and renewal in all living things. You will never be grown-up.

Grown-ups possess great passion for manipulating life, but less passion for living it. I think that's why we're so afraid of teenagers: You want to live as widely and as deeply as you can. You scare us because you take us to the edge, to those raw, pure spaces we vaguely remember before our lives became routine and homogenized. When you ask questions, something in your eyes demands utter honesty.

I guess your aliveness is too real for us, too present, so we try to take it away from you. We tell you that the edge is unsafe, uncertain, risky. We try to convince you that safety is what matters, and fill your heads with fantasies of life insurance (the only insurance you have is that all life ends). We ask you to trade your land on the edge, like the island of Manhattan, for a box of trinkets—shiny things like prestige, pensions, tenure, fame.

There is a quality, a soul of youth, that doesn't have much to do with how old you are. No one can define it: It's too deep and mysterious a thing to be captured in words. But you both have always been attracted immediately to people who live out of their youthful soul. It has everything to do with courage, risk, vulnerability, extremes. It demands authenticity, and is willing to suffer for it. It wants to be tested, and will find its tests where it will.

And this is what scares me: When society does not offer you formal occasions to test your souls, you will find your own. As much as we scream out against gangs, violence, teenage pregnancies and young people experimenting with drugs, these are all perversions of the young soul's need to find its power and place in the world. Rather than engage that soul, we have chosen to pretend it isn't there.

It's not that we're rotten people; we aren't. You've been around enough grown-ups to know that we generally mean well. It's just that we're lost right now. Identity crises don't just happen to individuals. Whole societies go through times when they lose their story and forget who they mean to be. We don't know how to initiate you because we ourselves were never initiated, and because we feel so out of control of the world that we don't know what we're initiating you into. That's why becoming a man is such a weird and troubling thing these days, why ten-year-olds carry guns and live like soldiers while forty-five-year-olds still play King of the Hill—only now it's at an office.

I still have trouble thinking of myself as your father. Your "dad," yes. That feels easy, comes naturally. Being a father sounds more serious, more solid and self-assured, more worthy of respect and admiration (and just a wee bit of fear) than I'll ever want or warrant. My image of a father is one who molds, corrects, approves. Dads buy tools they don't know how to use, become timers at swim meets just to be close to you, cry at piano recitals.

Still, our relationship is rigged: You two didn't exactly choose me as the male with whom to spend your impressionable years. So sometimes—usually in the middle of the night, when I sneak into your rooms just to hear the sound of your breathing as you sleep—I get to wondering. What if we weren't separated by a generation, or connected by our DNA? Would we be pals? I have this craving to find out what it would be like to be twelve years old together, for you to know me not as your dad, but as the boy I was when I passed through what you're passing through now.

So here is a story about the boy I was. Let's call it "The Boy Who Lived with a Beast in His Room":

Once upon a time there was a boy with a Beast in his room. The Beast came only at night, and only when he wasn't looking. Sometimes it would come through his door, and sometimes through his window, but because the door and the window were on different sides of the room, the boy could not watch both at once. The boy knew that the Beast meant to devour him, so he did not sleep much.

One morning, after another sleepless night, the boy's father found him looking pale and panicked at the breakfast table.

"What troubles you, son?" his father asked.

"There is a Beast who means to eat me at night," said the boy, and he told his father about the door and the window, and not being able to look in two directions at once. His father was quiet for a moment. Then he said, "We will make a cage for this Beast, you and I, and we will trap her in the cage and you will be rid of her for good."

So they did. The boy and his father built a sturdy cage out of the strongest things they owned. From the boy's baseball bats and fishing poles, his report cards and swimming medals, from his father's neckties and car keys, his wedding ring and the locks on his briefcase, they fashioned their cage, and set it in the boy's room.

That night, the boy watched the door, but the Beast came through the window. It picked up the smell of the boy from the cage, and entered it. And faster than fast, the boy leaped from his bed, slammed the door shut and locked it with triumph. The Beast was stunned, but only for a moment. Then, with a fierce wail, it raised itself up and with one sweep of its hairy paw, shattered the cage like glass.

The boy ran from his room and slept with his parents.

The next morning, it was his mother who spoke. "I have a feeling about your Beast," she said. "Perhaps he is simply starving and craves something to eat. If we made him something very special and left it for him as a gift, perhaps he would satisfy his hunger and trouble you no more."

So they did. They made the Beast a cake, the moistest, sweetest, most satisfying cake you can imagine. They iced it thickly, and set it on the boy's bed like an offering. Like a sacrifice.

That night, when the Beast arrived, it ate the cake. But its hunger was still not satisfied, and it came after the boy, too.

The next night, the boy gave up: He could live without sleep no longer. He lay on his bed and waited for the Beast to come and devour him. And it came, through the door this time.

The boy smelled it first, smelled its awful, fiery breath. Sparks flashed from its fur. There was no escape this time, and the boy felt his fear pounding through his veins like a drumbeat. Hypnotized, he rose from his bed and faced the Beast. With a courage that comes only in the presence of essential things, the boy did what others would not: He looked the Beast in the eyes.

In those red eyes, he saw the reflection of himself. And as the jaws of the Beast opened to devour him, the boy saw something else, something unexpected: A teardrop forming in the corner of one eye. The tear did not fall, but it was there.

The boy stepped forward to his fate. To his wonder, the Beast stepped back. The boy stepped back, and the Beast stepped forward. Wherever the boy stepped, so stepped the Beast. They moved together, the boy and the Beast. In time their movement became a dance.

Many years have passed. The boy is a man now, with sons of his own. Someday they will build cages for their beasts, or ply them with their own sweet cakes. And when these fail, as they must, the manbeast will come again to the darkness of his son's room, to devour or to dance.

I know you have both met your beast already. I know the look in your eye when you come to your mom and me in the middle of the night, frantic because you haven't been able to sleep. And I know the despair you feel when all we can tell you, as a trainer tells a prizefighter, is to get back into the ring. I once stood sweating at my parents' bedroom door, just as you now stand at ours. I hope you will remember that spot as the place where life first called you to adventure. It probably won't make sense to you now, but my life began in those sleepless nights when everything vanished except me and the Beast.

Sometimes your best teacher and most trusted friend comes wrapped in the skin of a monster. It will give me such pleasure to watch you dance with yours.

Love,
Dad

In another life, years ago, Elizabeth Chu Richter was a little girl grow-
ing up in Hong Kong, walking home from school every day through
Victoria Park, past the soccer players and the swimming pool and the
old people on benches, munching on curried squid or stir-fried clams she
bought from the street vendors at the park entrance. But then things
changed: Her father died, and a few years later her mother decided to
carry out their plans to emigrate to America, moving to Dallas, a
woman alone with six children, settling into a small duplex in a quiet
neighborhood. And everything was different: no streetcars, no jostling
sidewalk crowds, no servants cooking their meals, no strict nuns in the
classroom. Now she went to public school.

A sea change, and one that took some getting used to. But Richter,
now an architect in Corpus Christi, cherishes the duality of country and
culture, passing the gift of two worlds and two sensibilities to her chil-
dren, Elissa, sixteen, Michael, thirteen, and Maya, nineteen. Richter met
her husband, David, in architecture school, and found in him a soul
mate. "I don't look at him as being American and me Chinese," she says,
"because we have so much in common. We just have a little added spice
from my traditions, but the basics are the same."

Dear Maya, Elissa and Michael:

From the time your father and I first met at the University of Texas,
we talked of our families and the idea of family. We quickly learned that
though we were from different cultures and worlds, we shared everything important. Ideas about commitment, discipline, excellence and
hard work can cross all borders.

Your father saw in my family and traditions an opportunity to build
pride, clarity and a strong identity in our young family, and he quickly became what he likes to call "Chinese-in-law." I, on the other hand, was already quite "American," having lived in the U.S. since I was a young teen.

So why does the thought of writing a letter to my children bring tears
to my eyes and a hollow, pressing feeling deep in my stomach? Can it
be because once again I am reminded of our mortality, of a loss long

"My task was simple: I needed to build a family memory as strong as steel and as comforting as silk."
ELIZABETH CHU RICHTER

Elizabeth Chu Richter with her husband, Michael, and children Michael, Maya, and Elissa

ago, and losses yet to come? My father's sudden and early death at the age of thirty-nine has, no doubt, shaped my outlook on life. I was only nine, but the oldest of six children. This early experience with one of life's unpredictable twists made me realize how fleeting our time is, and that "togetherness" is an essence that can and will outlast our physical existence.

Knowing that I could not be with you always, my task was simple. I needed to build a family memory as strong as steel and as comforting as silk. I emphasized to you at a very early age the importance of your ties to each other. My mother has often told me that my brothers and sisters are like my arms and legs: an integral part of me. So I, too, taught you to value each other's company, and that as long as you have each other, you will never feel alone.

When you were young, the word *boring* was not allowed to exist in our house: You always entertained yourselves well. The countless hours the three of you spent together, swimming and playing tennis, sharing the delights and agonies of piano recitals, memorizing lines from the movies we watched, and traveling with our family to countries far away will become the glue that will bind you and warm your years later on, like a steaming bowl of chicken and octopus soup.

To give you strength, I cooked. Every evening, we feasted on traditional Chinese dishes, such as sour bamboo shoot and beef, or re-created foreign dishes we enjoyed on our travels together, such as tortilla española. At the dinner table, your minds were strengthened, too. Remember the many lively discussions we had, such as the one comparing scientific relativity with moral relativism? We decided that while we might join Einstein, dropping stones from a train, we would keep our family footings on absolutes. We ate for hours, we reminisced, we laughed, we sang and sometimes even cried. The clanging of the steel spatula against the blackened iron wok, the aroma of the sizzling garlic and black beans will remind you of your strength.

There were times when your peers challenged the parameters we imposed on you, which seemed strict to them. In fact, there were really but a few simple things, such as having respect for your elders and being a trustworthy, responsible person. Perhaps your ability to say "No, thanks" with confidence to your peers stemmed partly from our insistence that academics come first, and that marriage is not an option before college graduation. My approach to parenting is admittedly old-fashioned, but what has worked for 7,000 years is certainly worth a try.

My Chinese upbringing affirms that I will always be my mother's child. What a relief and blessing it is for me to know this; my mother, your "Po-Po," has given me such comfort. She always said, "When the drunken man has lost his horse, who is to know if it is his good fortune or bad?" It is one of my favorite sayings.

As we spin our silk threads, every now and then I am shaken by the passing of time, of the impending separation. I tell you, as I tell myself, to enjoy each stage of life. Do not be in a hurry. Savor the moments. Love your family passionately.

The years your father and I have with you are the Golden Years, the years when we were one. You will always be our children.

With all that is within us,
Mommy (and Daddy)

Business consultant Jay Abraham made a million dollars by the time he was thirty, but if you ask him about it, he will tell you, "It's not how old you were when you made your first million, but how old you were when you lost it." He was thirty-three. "You get humility and wisdom as you get older and make mistakes," he says. At the weekend training seminars Abraham offers in Southern California, participants pay as much as $15,000 for creative inspiration and advice on how to make their businesses more profitable. But many clients also consult the expert privately. His fee: $3,000 per hour.

In Indianapolis, where Abraham grew up, he learned from observing his parents — both their successes and their failures. They taught him to have compassion and respect for other people. But as a salesman, Abraham says, his father chose the security of working for someone else's company over achieving his own life goals. For his part, Abraham says, "I don't crave security. I have infinite confidence in my own ability to generate work, and to be whatever I want to be." Abraham lives in Palos Verdes, California, with his wife, Christy. Jordan, seven, is one of seven children.

Dear Jordan,

I set out to write you a letter that would teach you what I have learned. Ironically, I've probably learned more lessons from observing you than I'll ever be able to give you. But I want to try. I want to share with you so many important and wonderful life lessons I've been taught. In this, my forty-sixth year, I've experienced much more than my age would suggest. I think I can tell you a few simple things that you can easily understand. I hope they will make as big a difference to your life as they have to mine.

First, I wish I was so much more like you, my joyous young son. I enjoy the sparkling twinkle of your ever-focused, big brown eyes. I wish I had the curiosity about everything and everyone that you have. I do share your kindness, and, I think, your gentle, loving nature. But boy oh boy, do you know how to enjoy life.

"Nothing will change if you make a million dollars,
have a big house, and drive a Mercedes. Believe me,
I know. I've done that."
JAY ABRAHAM

Jay Abraham and son Jordan

Right now, you are seven, but soon you'll be older. Don't forget how much fun this time in your life has been. Recognize that most other kids and adults aren't as happy or secure as you are, and make it your job to connect with them. Everywhere you are, talk to the kids, not just the ones you know, but ones you don't know, particularly the ones who seem shy, or stay quietly in the corner by themselves. Get interested in them. Ask their names, where they live, what they like to do, what their favorite TV show is. You can always find a few spare minutes to make the effort.

Taking the time to talk to other kids or to play with them might seem like nothing, but it could be everything. Your interest and understanding at a critically formative time in their lives could change their very fate. Really it could! When someone takes an interest in you, when they nurture and encourage you, you gain confidence. You can give so many insecure and unhappy people confidence, happiness and a whole, fresh outlook on life just by being their friend.

I guess I'd better make sure you know the difference between a good person and a not-so-good person. Most people are naturally good. They don't always know how to show all their goodness, but it's there. Just because someone doesn't smile doesn't mean they don't want to. It just means no one ever taught them how it's done. You get to be the person who has the privilege of showing those people how to laugh, smile, talk and have fun. If you want someone to talk to you, talk to him first. If you wish kids would play with you, go up and play with them first. If you'd like them to smile at you, smile at them first.

I think most people go about their lives all wrong. They are told that they're here to get an education. To use that education to build a successful career. To use that successful career to build a successful marriage and family. And then to start the same, pressurized process all over again.

I totally disagree. I believe we're on this earth to savor the process. Here and now, at the wonderful, innocent age of seven years old, you can decide to preserve that same childlike freshness and fun-loving curiosity. It's a shame not to enjoy it forever, not merely for a few more years.

It's easier to enjoy life than not to enjoy it. Getting bored takes energy. You have to stop reflecting on all the fascinating things, people and places around you. Getting scared that you'll fail takes enormous effort, since man's natural tendency is to want to do things and try things. Anything else requires work, effort and tremendous energy. I don't know about you, but I always prefer pleasure to pain. So, I've tried to find pleasure and enjoyment in everything I did and everyone I met.

I love to listen. Again, I'm not in any hurry to get my words in. I want to learn what someone else sees or thinks that's different or the same as I do, and why they feel the way they do. It makes me grow. And growth is the essential ingredient in having a happy, powerful life.

This year you went from being a clumsy, awkward soccer player to a well-coordinated, scrappy athlete. But you shouldn't be content to just grow your body. Grow your mind and your heart and your mindset, too. Learn and discover as much information as you can about as many different things as you can. Learn about science. Read good books. Learn about sports and music and politics and philosophy. There's nothing that isn't fascinating if you want to learn.

Don't think that everyone looks at things the same way you do—they don't. You don't have to agree with them. But you do have to try to understand their point of view and respect how they see things whether you think it's right or not. Why? Because it's their reality. They may not have had a mother like yours to encourage them to experience life. They may not have had the money or opportunity to learn to swim or to play the games you play. They may never have felt as loved and wanted as you feel, Jordan. Their teachers may have been close-minded, fearful people, so that all they learned were close-minded thoughts. But don't ever condemn, belittle or make fun of people, Jordan.

Life secrets I have learned:

Everyone wants to be interesting, son. But the trick is to become "interested." When you're truly interested in others, you can't help but become the most "interesting" person anyone will ever meet.

Most people fall in love with themselves or their jobs or their career. I hope you'll fall in love with all the people you do things with or for in life.

Life isn't about achieving an end product. Nothing will change if you make a million dollars, have a big house on top of a hill, marry the most beautiful woman in town and drive a Mercedes. Believe me, I know. I've done that.

Don't take yourself too seriously, and, by all means, don't worry too much about what other people think or say. You're not that important and you shouldn't be.

When it comes to college and a career, do what you love, not what other people want you to do.

Marry if it's right. There's no place in real love for jealousy, selfishness or power struggles. There's unlimited room for understanding, appreciation, interest and encouragement.

Make time for your wife and your family, more time than I made for you and your brothers and sister.

I have the utmost confidence in you, son. But, if you ever need me, I'll always be there for you, by example, if not in person.

Lovingly,
Your Father

"You don't have to be accepted
by anyone but God."
STEVE POIRIER

Steve Poirier and son Nick

In the photograph, Steve Poirier's father is grinning broadly, a beer in one hand. This is the way Poirier likes to remember him, a man who, Poirier says, "was never a huggy-kissy kind of guy. My father was a very hard worker and a good provider and we children knew he loved us, but he never showed his emotions."

With his own son, Nick, six, the Greyhound bus driver wants to do things differently. Hugs are exchanged frequently, and father and son spend plenty of time together, playing baseball in their Houston neighborhood, running errands or watching videos on nights when Poirier isn't on his way to New Orleans or Brownsville or Texarkana, passengers in tow. "When I was growing up in the fifties, there seemed to be a whole lot less to worry about," he says. "The world is so dangerous now. I feel kind of helpless a lot of times." Religion helps him chart a steady course: As Jehovah's Witnesses, he and his wife, Dianne, study and pray several times a week at a Kingdom Hall. "The Bible tells you that man cannot guide his own footsteps," Poirier says. "I want Nick to put God first in his life and I want to show him how to do it."

Dear Nick,

When you were just over a year old, I began noticing how you copied many of the things I did. If I wore a baseball cap, you had to have one on. If I shaved, you had to lather up your face and pretend to use the razor. If I worked on the car, you had to get some tools so you could work on it, too. It made me realize what an awesome responsibility I had to set the right examples for you. I understand now why alcoholics often had alcoholic parents, and spouse abusers often had abusive parents: These things continue until someone breaks the cycle.

Every man wants a son to carry on his legacy. You're the son I always wanted. I only wish you had gotten here sooner. Tomorrow, I'll be forty-nine years old and you are just five. We're both healthy, but our age difference sometimes makes me wonder if I'll get to see you grow up. My father was only fifty-six when he died. Also, I'm out on the highway on a daily basis. I know that I'm a safe driver, and as far as it depends on me,

I'll be fine. But I can't depend on the drivers of other vehicles to do the right thing.

There are many different kinds of people in the world. I'm white and your mother is black, which puts you somewhere in between. But this says nothing about who you are. It only says two people from different backgrounds cared enough about each other to make you. Some people speak out against mixed marriages. They say things like, "The kids won't be accepted," or "They won't know what they are," or "Other kids will tease them." What a bunch of foolishness. You don't have to be accepted by anyone but God, and kids always find something to tease one another about.

You don't have to adopt anybody's culture. Enjoy any kind of music you like, eat the food you like, dress the way you like, and when you're grown and start to look for a wife, the only race you'll have to limit your search to is the human race. Don't allow yourself to be classified based on your ethnic background. Build character and a good reputation and let that define who you are.

They say education is the key. In order to be self-sufficient, you must have a job. In order to do the job, you must learn. But college is overrated. Four years of college convinced me that anyone with average intelligence, who has the time and money, can get a college degree. Sure, for certain occupations, college is required. But there is nothing wrong with working with your hands. Find a good, honest career that you enjoy, and be good at it.

I got into bus driving by accident. I was close to getting my bachelor's degree and was looking for a better job. I knew someone who went to work for Trailways Bus System. I heard that they were hiring and that the money was pretty fair so I went to check on it. That was sixteen years ago and I've never looked back.

Bus driving is not a job for someone who doesn't like all kinds of people. I interact with forty to eighty different people from every walk of life each day. I've had everybody on my bus from the White House staff to the poor guy using his last few dollars to buy a ticket to a city where he thought he could find a job. I've witnessed a lot of sad good-byes, but the happy reunions I've seen have more than balanced it out. I've seen some wonderful sights: the redwoods in California, Crater Lake in

Oregon, Mackinac Island in Michigan, Niagara Falls. I hope to go back to all these some day with you. I've driven my bus across the George Washington Bridge, the Golden Gate Bridge, and even the London Bridge, in Lake Havasu City, Arizona. I used to say I couldn't believe I was being paid to go on vacations. But the best part of my job has always been the people.

I especially liked doing trips with senior citizens. I remember Lola Larson wearing her tam with the pom-pom, and her traveling companion, Marge Ross. They came so often I kept a picture of them, so that when they didn't come, I could set it on the dashboard and everything would seem normal.

Then there was Claire Gorney, a short, plump woman with a round face and rosy red cheeks. She wore glasses and her hair was pulled back in a bun. She walked with a cane, but don't let that fool you. If you got in a footrace with her, you'd lose every time. I remember when we went to Colorado and she led the pack up Pikes Peak.

Senior citizens appreciate life more than youngsters. They want to squeeze everything they can into whatever time they have left. Your Grandma was the same way. If I was on a tour, and we were supposed to leave at 8:00 A.M., they'd be lined up at 6:00 A.M. waiting for the restaurant to open. After breakfast, they'd all put on their walking shoes and walk circles around the hotel. It looked like a track meet out there.

I would usually skip breakfast, opting for a little extra sleep and a cup of coffee to go. But they'd keep an eye out for me, and as soon as I headed for the bus, here they'd come like a herd of fertile turtles ready to go. I wouldn't take anything for the times I spent with them. The lesson is to learn to appreciate life at an early age. It is a gift.

One time, I took a garden club to Dallas for a convention. On the way back to Houston, we were to stop and visit a man who owned a peanut farm outside of Athens, Texas, and have lunch there. The lady in charge of the charter was reading the directions to me as we went along. We started out on the Interstate, went to a state highway, to a farm road, then got down to "Turn right at the blue house."

I ended up driving down a dirt road, and came to the top of a hill, a gentle downward slope with a six-inch layer of soft sand on top of a firm base. I told the lady in charge I could go down the hill, but I wasn't sure

I could make it back up again. She assured me the man we were going to see had a large tractor that could pull us out if we got stuck. We proceeded down the hill, took a sharp left at the bottom, and drove up a short driveway to the farmhouse.

When it was time to leave, I started up the hill again, but I couldn't build momentum, and we got stuck in the sand. One of the passengers headed back up the driveway to tell the farmer to bring his tractor, while we all piled out of the bus to wait. After a while, a "good ol' boy" in an old Chevy pickup truck came down the road towards us. He wore blue jeans, boots, and a baseball cap, and had a mouthful of chewing tobacco. "What are ya'll doing down here?" he asked. I said, "Isn't Dallas just up this road a ways?" He said, "No. Dallas ain't up that way. How are you going to get out of that sand?" I said: "They're sending one of those big helicopters out and it's going to lift the bus right out."

In a few minutes, the farmer arrived with his tractor, but for a long while, the bus just sat there, wheels spinning. I was wondering if we'd ever get back. I didn't want to be a bus driver anymore. I couldn't even call Greyhound to come get me because I had no idea how to tell them where I was. I could hear them saying, "Turn right at the blue house? Have you been drinking?" Finally, the farmer found the right gear and the tractor and bus moved slowly up the hill.

It's a funny thing about experiences like that one. I knew I shouldn't have gone down that hill. But in the end, things turned out all right and I had a good story to tell. Sometimes, on days when work isn't going so well, I think about that story and laugh, and that makes things seem a little better again.

Your mom has been doing a fine job working with you on your manners. Words like "please," "thank you," and "excuse me" will never go out of style. I'm glad you have a sense of humor. I don't know where you got that little temper from. We need to work on that. When you lose your temper, you often say and do things you later regret. Saying you're sorry won't erase the memory of what you said or did. In twelve years, your mom and I have never had an argument. Sometimes we disagree, but we know how to disagree without being disagreeable. Mom thinks I'm too easy on you and I know she's right. That's something that I have to work on.

Don't let your heroes be entertainers or athletes. I'm sure Hakeem the Dream and Clyde the Glide are wonderful people, but they're only men, and they make mistakes on a daily basis. Keep studying your book, *The Greatest Man Who Ever Lived*, and make Jesus your hero. He always set the perfect example. When you copy him you can't be wrong.

To sum it up, be honest and fair in all your dealings. Let your "Yes" mean yes and your "No" mean no. Don't be afraid of being different. Cultivate the fruitage of God's spirit—love, joy, peace, kindness, goodness, faith, mildness, self-control—and you will prosper.

I love you very much,
Dad

"Recipes are memory makers."
IBBIE LEDFORD

Ibbie Ledford and granddaughter Deidra

The best meal Ibbie Ledford ever ate, she says, was prepared by her mother: hog backbone and ribs boiled with lots of pepper and salt, served up with black-eyed peas and cornbread, for sopping up the juice. Cooking was a big part of life in Dyersburg, Tennessee, where Ledford grew up milking cows, gathering eggs from the henhouse, and peeling tomatoes for canning. When she was five, her father made her a wooden stool so she could reach the kitchen cabinets, to help her mother fix dinner. Later, Ledford's own children used the stool, and then her grandchildren, standing up tall to help her cut dough for cookies and biscuits. "If my house were to burn, I'd grab that little stool first," she says.

Shared stories and shared meals hold families together, Ledford believes, and both play a large role in her books, including Hill Country Cookin' *and* Memoirs *(Pelican Publishing, 1991). Deidra, sixteen, likes it when her grandmother bakes Aunt Clara's Lemon Chess Pie. Ledford herself eats and enjoys a wide variety of cuisines, but in the end, she says, "I'm just an old Southern girl, and I love Southern cooking."*

Dearest Deidra:

You're going to be sixteen years old! I can't believe it. You're turning into a woman before my eyes, even though you're often a child in my mind.

When you were born, Granddaddy and I didn't know if we'd be blessed with a granddaughter or grandson. I secretly hoped for a girl. There were so many things I longed to share with a granddaughter. I wanted a little girl in my kitchen again. The step stool your mother used before she was tall enough to reach the kitchen counter was waiting patiently.

The day of your birth was nothing like my own, sixty years ago, or so I hear tell. As I grew up, I often pestered my mother and my older sister, Margaret, to relate how I came into the world, and from them I learned how I came about. It was August 6, 1932, a typically very hot day here in West Tennessee. Mama and Aunt Ibbie were canning tomatoes. Mama was filling the last jars when a labor pain nearly knocked her to the floor. There were no telephones in the area, so Aunt Ibbie called for

Austin, the oldest, and ordered him to saddle up Hickorynut and ride to the store to bring back my father. Austin ran to the pasture, bridle in hand, scared to death he'd spook old Hickory and not be able to catch him. But somehow he managed to get him bridled. Leaving the saddle behind, he headed toward the store at a gallop.

The crops were already "laid by," so the menfolk were at Tickle's store, swapping stories, mule-trading and pitching horseshoes. Papa knew something was wrong when he saw Austin riding up. He quickly asked, "Is it Mama?" When Austin said yes, Papa asked Uncle John to take the truck the eight miles into town to fetch Dr. Turner.

Mama called Margaret to her bedside and told her to take the little ones to Mrs. Cleo's house. Late in the afternoon, Papa pulled into Mrs. Cleo's front yard blowing the horn. He jumped out of the truck with a big grin on his face. The kids ran into his arms and he enveloped them in a big bear hug and said, "Young'ns, you've got a pretty little baby sister, and we're namin' her after your Aunt Ibbie!" (That's always my favorite part of the story, Deidra.)

Aunt Ibbie worked all afternoon to prepare a scrumptious meal of fried chicken, gravy, mashed potatoes, butter beans, biscuits and lemonade. Lemonade was served only on special occasions. Dr. Turner took supper with the family, and left with a full stomach, a supply of Mama's canned vegetables, a large basket of tomatoes and potatoes, and the promise of $25.00 cash when the crops were harvested.

As the years passed, Deidra, I quickly learned how to find my way around the kitchen. Mama said that was one way we could show our love for people, especially our husbands and children. And I do that for you, too, when I prepare your favorite foods, especially your number-one favorite dessert: Aunt Clara's Lemon Chess Pie.

You've become a good cook, and best of all, you like doing it. I had my troubles in the kitchen, too. One morning, when I was ten, I skipped out of bed before anyone else was up with thoughts of surprising Mama on Mother's Day: I was going to cook breakfast for the whole family. Though I was still very young, I had helped Mama many times before in the kitchen, and felt sure I could manage all by myself.

The skillet I needed was hanging on the wall behind the stove. A grease can in which Mama stored fried meat grease was sitting on the stove right under that skillet. With the help of a kitchen chair I reached up and unhooked the pan. Made of iron, it was much heavier than I thought, and down it fell against the grease can, knocking it to the floor. Grease splattered all over the stove, cabinets, and floor. What a mess!

When Mama entered the kitchen a while later, I was down on my hands and knees trying to clean up with a towel. The grease on the floor caused it to shine as if it had been waxed. "Oh! You're so smart! You've scrubbed and waxed the floor!" Mama said. I burst into tears, and between sobs, told my pitiful story. Mama gathered me in her arms and said, "It's all right, honey. You can still cook breakfast and I'll help you, just like you often help me. Tell me what to do and we'll get started."

I voted for flapjacks. The first two or three didn't turn out very well, and after a while Mama subtly guided me to an easier chore for a ten-year-old, asking if I planned for us to eat in the kitchen or the dining room. I immediately offered to set the dining room table, and jumped up from my chair, leaving the flapjacks to Mama. She proceeded to prepare a delicious breakfast, all the time asking my advice and making me feel I was in charge.

When everything was ready, Mama remarked what a treat it was to have someone cook breakfast for her on Mother's Day. She made me very happy that day, turning Mother's Day into Little Girl's Day.

As you can tell, Deidra, I grew up in an age quite different from the one in which you live. But the human virtues of love and honesty are always a must in order to live a good life. In today's culture, it has become more difficult to express these virtues, but you've been able to struggle through with flying colors. I'm so proud of my granddaughter. Mama and Papa would have been proud of you, too.

Hugs and Kisses,
Granny

P.S.: Here's the recipe for Aunt Clara's Lemon Chess Pie. Recipes are memory makers. I hope you'll bake up a batch of wonderful memories for you and yours to enjoy.

AUNT CLARA'S LEMON CHESS PIE

1 deep-dish unbaked pie crust

4 eggs

2 cups sugar

1/4 cup butter or margarine, melted

1 tablespoon flour

1 tablespoon cornmeal

1/4 cup milk

1/2 cup lemon juice

1 tablespoon grated lemon peel

In large mixing bowl, beat eggs. Set aside. Mix flour and cornmeal with sugar. Add to eggs, mixing well. Stir in milk, lemon juice, melted butter and lemon peel. Pour into an unbaked pie shell. Bake in a 350-degree oven 45 minutes or until brown and set.

In the town of Berne, Indiana, you can listen to a yodeler, eat bratwurst at the annual Swiss Days festival, admire the neatly manicured lawns and spotless downtown streets, or learn about the Mennonites and Amish who farm in the area. But perhaps the most unusual aspect of this small town, founded in 1835 by Swiss immigrants, is the conservative—some might say old fashioned—ethic of its citizenry: Hard work, church, and family remain as important to many families as they were a century ago.

Charles Isch is a good example. He started as a teller at the First Bank of Berne thirty-one years ago, working his way up to president. The bank, Isch says, is known for providing award-winning service with half the employees of most institutions its size, charges no mortgage fees, and until a few years ago, had not foreclosed on a borrower in fifty years. Families in Berne stay close together, and Isch and his wife, Linda, are no exception: Four generations of their extended family live in and around town, a tradition of closeness the banker would like to in-still in his grandchildren, one-year-old Garrett and two-year-old Brian and Rowan.

Dear Brian, Rowan and Garrett:

I don't know when you'll get around to reading this letter. You older two are just now learning to talk. Garrett, you're so new I'm still just starting to get to know you.

You probably know by now that I'm not the kind of person who writes a lot of letters. For most of my life, almost all of my family and friends, as well as Grandma's, have lived right here, within a few miles of our house.

For almost a month now, I've been thinking about what I want to say to you kids. First of all, I hope you will grow up to be hard workers. When your parents played on the same Little League team, I used to hit them grounders just about every night when I got home from work. When I was teaching them to play basketball, we shot hundreds of free

"All the financial advice I've given over the past thirty years can be boiled down to one sentence: Don't spend more than you make."
CHARLES ISCH

Charles Isch and grandsons Rowan and Brian

throws up in the hay mow. Every summer, we ran up and down the stone road to get ready for the Swiss Days Race.

I've always believed that in sports, hard work could make up for just about any shortcoming. Your Uncle Brent is probably the best example of this. He's not very tall, but he played center on his high school football team, a position ordinarily played by much bigger guys. And you know what? Simply because he worked hard, both physically and in learning everything he could about the game, Brent made All-State.

I think the same thing is true in life. If you work hard, you will get ahead. This is something I learned from my dad. Not from anything he said so much as just watching what he did, how he and his brothers lived their lives. Dad never made a lot of money farming, so in the mid-'50s he also started working in the produce department of a grocery store in Berne. It wasn't a high-paying job. But because he's always worked hard and lived frugally, he's been able to live comfortably in retirement. (Of course, Great-Grandpa has never completely retired. Even now, at eighty-two, he still mows that huge yard at the church.)

I don't think my dad ever really considered not working hard. Like so many Swiss people who live in and around Berne, hard work is just part of his heritage, and part of mine. I never dreamed I would work in a bank, much less become the president of one. I always thought I'd be a farmer. But after Dad sold his cows, farming wasn't really an option for me anymore. So I decided to go to business school.

Those first few months, I hated getting on that bus to Fort Wayne every Sunday night. I missed being on the farm. In the spring, during planting season, sometimes I'd catch a ride home on a weeknight just so I could drive a tractor for a few hours. I'd only been out of school a few months and was working for a food company in Fort Wayne when the vice president of the bank went to see Dad at the grocery store. He wondered if I would come work for them. I think the main reason I got the job was that the vice president knew what a hard worker my dad was.

Let me tell you something, though: There's no way I would have become president of the bank if I hadn't worked very, very hard, too, for thirty years. I don't just mean long hours, either. I always did the extra things, little jobs other people didn't want to take on. I spent a lot of time thinking about how I could do my job better, how the bank could be better.

Your parents are hard workers, too. Rowan, that's how your mom became an award-winning reporter before she decided to become a full-time mom. Brian and Garrett, that's how your dad became his company's top salesman. It doesn't matter much to me whether you kids make a lot of money, or have fancy job titles. But whatever you do, I hope you try to do the best job you possibly can. That doesn't necessarily mean you'll get a promotion you think you deserve, or that you won't get laid off. But you will never be out of a job for long.

The second thing I want you to remember is something I learned from the older guys at the bank when I was just starting out: Don't spend more money than you make. Sometimes I think all the financial advice I've given over the past thirty years can be boiled down to that one simple sentence. This doesn't mean you should never borrow money. But if you consistently want more than you have or can afford, you will never be happy. And more than anything, I want you kids to be happy when you grow up.

This was probably easier for me to learn than it will be for you. Growing up on the farm, without TV, I didn't see a lot of commercials for toys and candy and so forth. About the only time I had money to spend was on Saturday night, when we went to town to get groceries and supplies. My dad would give my brothers and me each a dime. I'd buy a bag of cashews, or maybe a Lone Ranger comic book.

Sometimes people who didn't have much growing up try to make up for it later by spending money on themselves and their families, whether they can afford it or not. Credit card companies make a lot of money off of these people. You'd be surprised how many people owe thousands of dollars to credit card companies. I've seen loan applications listing $20,000, $50,000, even, in one case, $100,000 in credit card debt. These people are always trying to catch up, but few of them ever will.

Personally, I never felt deprived as a kid. My favorite memories don't have anything to do with money. Like the big family picnics we used to have at the state park. To make sure we'd have enough picnic tables, some of us boys would "reserve" them by sleeping on them the night before. We'd stay up late, talking and playing.

Your grandma and I have more money now than when your parents were kids, and we like to buy you things. You already have more toys and clothes than I ever did. But I hope when you look back on your childhood, your favorite memories are things like playing kickball with your cousins, or swimming in the pond over at Great-Grandpa and Grandma Isch's house.

I've referred to our family several times in this letter. You guys may not realize how lucky you are to be growing up in a family that isn't scattered all over the country. It means that help is always nearby. Everybody in this family contributes in one way or another: Rowan, your mom is a writer, and I often ask her to look over my press releases and some business letters. But neither she nor your dad know much about working on houses, so your Uncle Brent and I have been giving them advice on how to strip your living room floor.

Maybe by the time you read this, you'll be starting to form an idea of what roles each of you will play. But mainly, I want you kids to think of your family as your friends, as I do. The people you call when you want to do something fun, or when you need help, or when you just feel like talking.

Love,
Grandpa

"The moments you and your dad share are special.
Take it from someone who longed for that."
BILL McKENNA

Bill McKenna with Kevin Sturino

Bill McKenna starts his workday at 6:45 A.M., sorting out the letters and the flats, the catalogs and the magazines, bringing order to the chaos of paper that floods into the Westmont, Illinois, Post Office each day. McKenna's father was a postal worker, as was his grandfather before that. When he graduated from college, his mother reminded him that the Postal Service offered job security and reasonable pay, and he decided to take the entrance exam. "I like my job," says McKenna, twenty-five years later. "It's fairly routine, but I like being outside delivering mail. It's like having two or three hours to yourself to think about anything you want to think about."

Ask him to recall the most important piece of advice he's ever received, and McKenna remembers something he once read: "You can never do a kindness too soon, because you'll never know how soon it will be too late." "It made me think about what my purpose is in life," he says. His father, though a harsh disciplinarian, was the same way, he says, taking an interest in people, trying to help out if he could. Kevin Sturino, five, lives next door to McKenna and his wife, Wanda.

Dear Kevin:

Sometimes as I watch you from my kitchen window I marvel at how much energy and enthusiasm a child of your age can generate. You certainly love your baseball.

You have progressed at such a rapid pace since I first observed you two years ago, when you barely could hold a bat. You are now swatting those plastic baseballs clean over our fence; your father, Jim, retrieving them so you can do it all over again and again.

You are very lucky to have a dad who on most summer evenings finds time to play baseball with his son. He talks to you constantly, using baseball vernacular, so that you become acquainted with all facets of the game. When my wife, Wanda, and I were over visiting with your folks recently, you surprised us by naming the entire Chicago Cubs starting lineup. Wow! A four-year-old Harry Caray in our midst! It is evident to both of us what a healthy interaction exists between you and your dad.

As for myself, the one-to-one relationship you experience with your dad was not possible in my formative years. My father, who passed away in November 1994, was busy most of his life trying to support a family of nine children—six girls and three boys—on a Post Office salary. My mother was just that: a mother who stayed home and worked from sunrise to sunset doing everything a good mother does.

I'm forty-five now, Kevin, and I have done a lot of reflecting since my dad's passing. I get particularly emotional when I see a movie depicting a special bond between father and son. I always feel somewhat cheated, wishing I, too, could have had a relationship with my father of a more intimate nature. He was a very stern individual who would not tolerate any nonsense or disrespect from his children. We had to say "Yes, sir" and "Yes, ma'am." We had curfews. He wouldn't allow back talk, and if you challenged him, it wouldn't do any good. The result was that I didn't ever feel I could talk to him about things that bothered me. His own father was much the same way, always making sure control was never wrested from his hands.

I guess the sheer number of children in our family required an almost military-type existence, so order could be maintained. In looking back, I guess there were just too many mouths to feed. My father truly had his hands full.

To my best recollection, the cohesiveness we had as a family was best reflected in three areas: evening meals, saying prayers together after the dishes were cleaned, and going to church on Sundays.

I remember being across the street one evening at my golf instructor's house when my dad yelled at the top of his voice for me to come home for dinner. This was particularly embarrassing as I was engrossed in learning what would become my favorite pastime. I did not want to leave. Mr. Tex Guillory, my golf teacher and friend, laughed and said, "The old man is really hot, Billy. You had better be on your way."

My dad was a very religious person. I guess we spent roughly twenty minutes each evening saying the rosary together as a family. He made each of us take turns reciting the mysteries of faith. Some of us fell asleep occasionally, only to be rudely awakened when he spotted us.

On Sundays, we usually needed a full pew in the church to accommodate our large family. Afterwards, my father delighted in showing off all his children to the other parishioners.

In his own way, my father loved and cared for each of us, although I was not endeared to his harsh methods. He instilled in us strong Christian values such as honesty, a sense of fairness, discipline, respect for the rights of others, and a strong work ethic. It is values such as these that he left us with, values, I may add, that are often sorely lacking in today's fragmented society.

So in a nutshell, what I guess I'm saying to you is to realize what a beautiful and precious situation you have. You have a father who finds time on most days to play baseball with you. He makes sure not only that you understand the game, but that you enjoy yourself along the way. The moments you share together are special. Take it from an outside observer who secretly longed for that.

Sincerely yours,
Bill McKenna

"Some customers you get really fond of; some
you can't get near no matter how hard you try."
DEBBIE FLYNN

Debbie Flynn with daughter Lisa

At Jason's Restaurant, just outside St. Louis, the meatloaf is homemade, the waitresses are apt to call you "Hon," and on your birthday, a six-ounce sirloin is on the house. It's the kind of place where senior citizens gather for morning coffee, and families pack the teal-and-white booths for "all-you-can-eat" dinners. Steve and Jerrold Rosenblum, Jason's owners, are known for their good deeds: donating food for the homeless, providing employment for disabled workers, catering youth program events for free.

Debbie Flynn has worked at Jason's for almost ten years, a short-timer compared with other members of the staff. "I enjoy being a waitress," she says. "It's been my life, really." Her daughter, Lisa, is sixteen. Says Flynn: "She's a pretty good kid, especially when I've had a long day."

Dear Lisa,

It's time for you to get out in the working world. It's not easy to work and go to school. I know. I had to do it when I was your age. I had to drop out of school to get a job when I was sixteen, because my dad had lost his, and I had to help support the family until he got back on his feet.

At first, I started working at a Steak & Shake as a cook on the line. Then I became a waitress. To be a waitress, you need to enjoy working with the public. The job can be challenging, but it's also fun. You have to know how to take care of people, how to make them want to come back. If there's no customers, there's no money. You need to treat people with respect.

Now I work for Jason's Restaurant. It's a good place to work, and all in all, I like my job. We have our ups and downs here, but we get through the days. Some customers you get really fond of; some you can't get near no matter how hard you try. I look forward to seeing our "regulars," like the "Hot Rod" Girls, Marie and Theresa, two sisters in their sixties who come in at least three times a day. We gave them the nickname because they drive a little brown TransAm. They always split an order of two eggs, toast and hash browns.

Then there's Cliff, the cabdriver. We hit it off pretty good: He's a friendly guy. Cliff always says, "There's nobody out on the streets, so I might as well come in and see all the waitresses." He usually orders our number 5, which is French toast, eggs and bacon. He likes to travel, visiting his grown kids around the country. When he comes back, we always ask him where he's been, and he tells us everybody's doing okay.

Sometimes, customers can be pains. One day when it was really busy, the customer I was waiting on stood up in the middle of the dining room and told everyone that he didn't want me to wait on him because I was white. That upset me, because I usually get along with everyone I wait on.

But that was really the only bad experience I've had over the years. I try to keep a sense of humor. If somebody's in a real hurry, for example, I'll say, "There's a McDonald's down the street." Still, being in my kind of business can be hard and stressful, especially when we're short-handed, when the cook doesn't show up, or a waitress is sick.

Over the years, I have worked a lot of hours, so I really haven't been able to spend as much time with you as I wanted. But I think you understood. Now you're getting some experience yourself, setting up trays in the back of the restaurant. I know you think it's easy. But someday you'll realize how hard it is waitressing out in front.

I'd like for you to finish school, to go to college. But you never know what you'll end up doing. Having a job like mine helps you become a better person. Once, a couple came in and she had lost her job, and they were thinking about separating because he couldn't handle it. I told them just to take it day by day, that things would work out. And they're still together, so maybe because of my job I helped them.

I hope you enjoy life as I have and that you help people as you can. Someday in the future you will understand what living is all about. It's not fun and games, as most kids today think.

Love,
Mom

Sid and Edith Schwartz may be retired and living in Florida, but don't ever call them "beach people." "I don't even go to the pool," says Edith, seventy-nine. Instead, the couple prefer playing bridge and canasta, taking in a concert or a show, going out to eat on the weekends with friends. After fifty-eight years of marriage—and almost as long as business partners—they have learned to respect each other's needs and habits, to be intimate without crowding, to divide tasks harmoniously.

As newlyweds, they struggled through the Depression, when jobs and money were scarce. Now the Schwartzes live comfortably, but their happiness, they say, comes from less material pleasures, such as visits with their grandchildren, Daniel, twelve, Adam, twenty-two, and Jessalyn, nine. "We're calm people," says Edith. "We aren't envious or jealous: We're satisfied with our lot in life. And we never get bored."

Dear Jessalyn, Daniel, and Adam:

Now that Grandpa and I have accumulated 160 years of living between us, it seems a fitting time to share with you some of our life's experience.

I have heard many youngsters talk about their need for "space," their desire for immediate gratification of their material needs, their unhappiness over relationships once glamorous, now turned sour.

These do not reflect the feelings Grandpa and I have had in our upbringing, our fifty-eight years of marriage and our current retirement. Ours has been a glorious partnership, one which started when we were mere children, saw us through the Great Depression, through family crises and bereavements, through a most painful separation and physical injury during World War II, and through a struggle to make a good and productive life for ourselves and our child, Jeff, your dad.

Partnership. That is the key word in our lifestyle. Our marriage started off modestly: a ceremony in the home of Grandpa's parents on January 16, 1938. Refreshments were sandwiches, salads, desserts, and drinks served to family and friends. Money was very tight then, so

"Call it fate or God or whatever. Someone
was watching over him for me."
EDITH SCHWARTZ

Sid and Edith Schwartz

Grandpa and I paid for the wedding. Grandpa's salary was the princely sum of $25 a week, for which he worked as much as sixteen hours a day.

No vine-covered cottage for us! We lived with my in-laws for two years until Grandpa was earning $40 a week. We were then able to get our own apartment and really start our life together. To us, the little apartment was our palace, even though it was tiny and we could only afford to furnish the bedroom.

Eventually, we moved to a more "luxurious" existence. Finances improved, and Grandpa, always thoughtful, would bring me a present on the sixteenth of each month, our anniversary day: candy, flowers, silk stockings—nylon was not invented till much later.

Then came World War II, and Grandpa and I served as air raid wardens together until his induction into the Army in 1943. With much sadness and many tears, we were parted. I would not let him see our house being packed up and stored for the duration. To spare him, I did it with the mover after he left.

While Grandpa served in the States, I followed him from one base to another, each time obtaining employment, settling down and then being uprooted when Grandpa was transferred. But it wasn't all sadness and sorrow. In my travels I met some wonderful people whose kindness I shall always cherish.

Right before Grandpa was shipped overseas, he got a pass for a "good-bye" visit to the family. We were driving back after midnight to his base from a party at my parents' house when our car, an old Buick with a honeycomb radiator, broke down near Clinton, New Jersey. Grandpa was due back by reveille the next morning, otherwise he would be declared AWOL. We knocked on doors, but no one would help us. I was chased by a very big dog—thank goodness he was on a chain! Cars passed driven by Army personnel, but they did not stop to help us, even though Grandpa was in uniform. Finally, Grandpa ended up taking a bus back to camp, and I found a guest house to stay in. The woman who poked her head out the upstairs window at 2:30 A.M. let me in because I looked so tired and forlorn. It turned out she had a son overseas, and she listened to my tale of woe, and fixed me a big breakfast the next morning: eggs, bacon, toast, fresh orange juice and coffee.

After Grandpa was shipped out, I went back to New Jersey, and decided to become an entrepreneur. I opened a small ladies' shop in Rutherford and called it The Clara May Dress Shop, since that was the name of my parents' store in Belleville. I took over the buying for both stores so that my mom would not have to work so hard.

The war years were very trying. Grandpa and I wrote every day, but mail delivery was erratic. The crushing blow was when I found that he had been injured. He spent four months confined to bed in an English hospital. Later, I learned that he and another GI had been ordered to bring a wounded man to the medics. During the time they performed this duty, their entire unit was wiped out. Call it fate or God or whatever. Someone was watching over him for me.

After his recuperation and the war's end, he visited the concentration camps in Germany. This was a traumatic event for him. He can never erase these scenes from his mind, and the Holocaust will live with him forever.

Upon his return, Grandpa resumed his old job, but the firm he worked for was liquidated, and he found himself jobless. In addition, there was now another mouth to feed in the Schwartz family: Much to our joy, your dad was born to us in November 1948, ten years after our wedding. No child was ever more welcome, as we had almost resigned ourselves to being childless.

So, there we were, a family, but Grandpa was unemployed. My little dress shop was flourishing, however, so I suggested to him that he work in the shop, too. He always had good taste and a sense of style. When he agreed, we really put our partnership to the test.

We decided to expand our horizons and rent another, larger store in a business section. We turned it into a small department store, and carried hosiery, gloves, handbags, jewelry, scarves, hankies, sweaters, blouses, jeans, slacks, skirts, dresses, suits, coats, robes and rainwear. So, you see, there was plenty of work to do.

We never discussed business at home. Home meant love, family, music, art, food and humor. In this way, we were able to spend twenty-four hours a day together without acrimony. We never tired of one another's company, for we shared common goals and a willingness to compromise.

In 1984, we decided to retire. As always, the decision was mutual. We sold our business and our house and moved to a lovely community in Florida. We had one advantage over many of our neighbors who found togetherness in retirement difficult to handle: To us, the partnership was merely a continuation and we didn't need to make any adjustments.

We share the housework and shopping, but, most of all, we share a common philosophy handed down from my parents: Never to be too busy to lend a helping hand. We try to make compassion and understanding a daily part of our lives. These, coupled with our mutual respect and love of family, continue to make our partnership as healthy and vital today as when we ran our business.

We love you all very much and wish you health, happiness and success in all your endeavors, and we wish for you the joy we have known in the partnership Grandpa and I share.

Love,
Grandma

"Never, *never* lead a charge in a mudball fight!"
VANCE VANNOTE

Vance Vannote and grandsons Matt, Joey (foreground), and Joshua

When Vance Vannote, a counseling psychologist, and his wife, Michele, a school principal, moved back to Fargo, North Dakota, in 1974, they saw a newspaper listing for a four-bedroom, green-and-white house on a tree-lined street. "That sounds like the house I grew up in," said Vance. It was, and the couple promptly settled in. Twenty years later, with their children grown, the Vannotes have the place to themselves, sipping coffee on the porch outside the bedroom on summer mornings, or standing by the vertical radiator in the kitchen to warm up during the long winters.

Few people move to Fargo for the climate. But there are other lures: Life is less hurried, people know their neighbors, the schools are good, and the Minnesota lake country is just a short drive away. In some ways, it hasn't changed all that much since Vance was growing up, going to Boy Scouts, fishing for walleye and northern pike with his Uncle Ed, snowballing a car or two, and collecting a few stories to pass on to his grandchildren, Joey, three, Matt, two, and Joshua, one.

Dear Joshua, Joey, and Matt:

We have a tradition at our house. During the summer, in the early evening, I sit at the dining room table doing something—writing a letter, reading a book, completing the monthly bills, or any of a number of other tasks—while your grandmother mows the yard. In my peripheral vision, I see her head going back and forth outside the open window as she does the boulevard on the north side of the house.

The mower normally is loud and annoying, but it's nothing compared to the racket it makes when she hits the steel pipe. The pipe, which sticks up above the ground about two inches, is owned by the city and I'm not sure what its purpose is. Every five or six years, city workers come along, unscrew the cap, poke a long stick down it to take some kind of measurement, engage in what appears to be about fifteen minutes of casual conversation, and then leave in their city truck. If it's noontime, sometimes they sit cross-legged around the pipe as if it has some ceremonial significance and have lunch before they return to the truck for a nap.

Anyway, your grandmother goes by the window, back and forth, back and forth. She likes to hit the pipe about once every two years, on average. It creates a tremendous racket, followed by a sudden, deafening silence. Sometimes, she breaks the mower and we can get it fixed; other times she demolishes it, sending parts all over the yard, and we have to get a new one. What's very interesting is that she leaves the mower, or what's left of it, on top of the pipe and walks into the house like nothing has happened, never saying a word about it. Just goes about her business in the kitchen or walks upstairs to watch TV or picks up a book and starts to read.

Meanwhile, the mower sits there on the pipe, languishing in the summer sun or weeping in the evening rain like an abandoned beanie with a broken propeller. Finally, I go out, lift the jilted machine off its scarred, victorious impaler and lug it off for repairs or a trade-in. For my part, I don't say anything about it either. With every fiber and living cell in my body I want to shout: "I don't care how unmechanical you are! When a mower blade hits grass, it cuts it. When it hits a steel pipe, it wrecks it. What is so difficult to understand about that?"

On the other hand, if I raise the mower-pipe issue, hackles would be raised, and I would surely end up mowing the grass myself. And as much as my fibers and living cells hate repressed emotional expression, they hate yard work even more. Sometimes, boys, you have to know when to avoid an argument in order to stay friends. This getting along with other humans is a perplexing business.

My earliest memories of "conflict resolution," as they say nowadays, involved a dispute with a neighborhood kid by the name of Willie Williams who lived across the street. I've long since forgotten what the dispute was about, but I thought I was grievously wronged in some manner. Well, one thing led to another, and a call to arms went out on both sides of the street. The Mother of All Neighborhood Mudball Fights was arranged and the details negotiated. In preparing my cache of mudballs, I recall making one in particular packed firmly around a fat, juicy worm, with Willie's name written all over it.

"Charge!" The word rolled out of my mouth just as a mudball flew into it. Nothing I have ever done, read, or heard before or since had such a dramatic impact on my opinions about resolving disagreements.

(Parenthetically, I also made some quick conclusions about the down-side of leadership.)

Blowing mucus and mud out of my nose, I reached for my ultimate weapon: the living, worm-filled mudball. I prayed that God was on my side, and that He would provide the spiritual and mechanical guidance needed for it to find that little heathen's mouth. (Willie and his family didn't go to church.) You know: an eye for an eye, a tooth for a tooth, a mud mouth for a mud mouth!

To this day, God still does not answer all my prayers in a fashion I would see fit. Thrown with all my might, the mudball sailed over Willie's head and shattered the kitchen-nook window of the Williamses' house. Later, I was to learn from my mother that the ball came apart on impact, thus freeing the worm, which continued through the broken windowpane and into the breakfast bowl of milk and oatmeal just that moment being consumed by an amazed Mrs. Williams.

Actually, Mrs. Williams was not only amazed but also enraged, and she burst through the front door, out into the battlefield.

She was a huge Scandinavian woman of enormous proportions. Im-mediately, all our playmates, as Louis L'Amour might have put it in one of his books, "headed out for friendlier parts." It occurred to me, hang-ing by the scruff of my neck from one of her large hands while Willie dangled from the other, that we would have been far better off dis-cussing our little misunderstanding quietly between ourselves. Some-times you should talk things over to solve a problem, and sometimes, as between your grandmother and me, you should just let it go.

Thinking about my troubles with Willie reminds me of another boy from my past: Lemonhead. Three things you should know. For a fifth grader, Lemonhead had an astonishingly sour disposition. He was un-questionably a brilliant debater. And he could play marbles like nobody you've ever seen.

Lemonhead could clean out a kid's lifetime accumulation of marbles in a single recess period—I mean, moonies, steelies, boulders, every-thing! I never saw him lose a game of marbles. I never heard him lose an argument. And I never knew him to keep a friend.

To keep a good relationship or friendship, I think you have to find a way to work out differences. You have to be able to lose a fight without losing your dignity. Just as important, and maybe more so, you have to be able to win a fight without causing the loss of dignity. And you can't win all the time. If you do, it will mean that around you, your friend can only be a loser, and if he's healthy he'll leave you to find a better friend.

So Joey, Joshua, and Matt, try to keep most of your marbles, but lose some now and then. Talk it over, but learn when to keep your trap shut, and never, *never* lead a charge in a mudball fight. If you want wisdom like this from anyone else but your Grandpa, they'll call it therapy and it'll probably cost you a lot of money.

Love,
Grandpa Vance

How to nurture another person's growth without interfering. How to be together yet separate. How to provide safety without locking any doors. These are the riddles that confront the psychotherapist and the parent as well. They are questions that Dr. Leston Havens has puzzled over for many decades, in his work as professor of psychiatry at Harvard Medical School, in his books—Learning to Be Human, A Safe Place, and others—and in raising his children.

Many of the most important lessons in life, Havens believes, come from making mistakes. "We are sustained by the nice things people say to us, but most of the time we learn from bumping up against things, from stubbing our toes." Most mornings, the psychiatrist can be found in the second-floor study of the Cambridge house he shares with his wife, Susan Miller-Havens. Reading has always been his passion, especially the novels of Joseph Conrad, whom Havens terms "a supreme psychologist." Havens's youngest daughter, Emily, is seventeen.

Dear Em:

A woman young, but still almost twice your seventeen years, told me she wanted to die. She said it quietly, as if she were speaking to herself. The world fell away outside, the cars on the street, the wind in the trees, as we contemplated that remark. She had drawn me into a space occupied by the idea of death.

I had just met her. A telephone message, a returned call, directions to my office, a few words of greeting, and then her remark: "I want to die."

Many years before, a patient I had known for several months said that something had changed. For as long as she remembered she had woken up and begun to plan her death. This she had never told me. Then, for the last week, she said, it had stopped; she no longer wanted to die. At the moment I was realizing her despair, she was telling me her hope. But not this patient.

"I'm sorry," I said. "I'm sorry you feel that." "No," she said, "since I decided I can die, it has been better. I do not have to bear my life anymore.

"You stand with your back to the light,
letting yourself be seen, but not calling attention."
LESTON HAVENS, M.D.

Leston Havens and daughter Emily

I've never talked about wanting to die with anyone. I waited a long time because it didn't seem fair to ask another person to listen."

She told me every relationship ended badly. She hated her work; she hated her body. Her only friend criticized her. Sometimes, watching a movie or reading a book, she forgot herself, but the same thoughts always returned: hatred of herself and now of her whole life.

We sat silently together for what seemed an eternity. I wanted to reassure her or rush her off to a hospital or speak more of the sadness. But nothing seemed right. I have learned to wait at such moments until the static of desperation leaves my mind. I wanted to respond with something that arose respectfully out of a sense of her feelings and my hope. I found myself saying, "Thank you for telling me. I wouldn't want you to bear that alone."

So often the worst difficulties spring from the best qualities. She had started life as an enthusiastic, open person, willing, even eager to help anyone. Her mother gave her a sort of Cinderella role in their large, poor family. Later, in school, she was scapegoated by a once-beloved teacher and still later in music school, a professor encouraged her, became intimate, then attacked her when the work she did diverged from his. She was always busy. Her competence and generosity attracted tasks; their number, and her thoughtfulness, were exhausting.

Perhaps it was this openness and receptivity that gave others the freedom to criticize her; she seemed to issue a hunting license to people. The young woman could not recall a single person who had encouraged her in a consistent and sustained way.

I believe this set my task. I have never seen a significant accomplishment that does not have behind it the encouragement and commitment of others. Over and over again I have found that those who claimed to make it alone had behind them parents or friends whose adoring voices were firmly planted in their heads. And those who do not have adoring voices too often hear critical ones, stopping them cold in their tracks.

The task came naturally to me because I admired her generosity and competence and the promise of her long-buried gift. It did not come easily because for many months my encouragement and praise met disbelief—simple, blank disbelief. I had to acknowledge her despair while somehow staying confident, or else she would not know that I knew how hard it was for her.

Medications helped. But there appears to be no lasting substitute for success itself. I believe our brains do not recognize the true possibilities open to them until they have lived a while in fresh circumstances. She needed to know that what she did not believe could in fact happen: the arrival of a new world that had to be built brick by brick. For her, it was a transformation from despair to hope, to the existence of changed possibilities. For me it was a privilege: to be present at the creation. Going forward, falling back, little by little she recovered the will to live, then the old talent, until finally she had constructed a livable existence.

I tell you this story, Emily, most of all because you helped me stay the course, simply by being yourself. Do you know the person you are? Let me say it directly: You stand with your back to the light, letting yourself be seen, but not calling attention; it is a gift given, but not given away— so like your mother. I have also watched you listen; your mind takes the world in to a place at once vibrant and settled. It is as if you draw a line around the other person and yourself, so that something real can happen between you. My patient is better at that now.

I also tell you the story because you, too, may sometimes despair, especially if, as I hope, you set goals that will always seem a little beyond you. I want you to know that despair is best spoken, best shared; that it is best divided and apportioned between yourself and someone to be trusted, because no one does anything important alone. I often wish I could be the one you share it with. That may not be possible, so there is another reason for this letter. I want to describe you to yourself, in order that these words may enter your mind, my belief in you, to remain there, a light for the dark times that reach us all.

Love,
Dad

Devotions

"I decided to turn my hatred into the more positive force of persistence."
MYRLIE EVERS-WILLIAMS

Myrlie Evers-Williams with grandson Daniel Medgar Evers-Everette

June 11, 1963, was a humid night in Jackson, Mississippi. Myrlie Evers let her children stay up late to watch President Kennedy's speech. When her husband, civil rights activist Medgar Evers, came home, he would spend some time with them, tuck them into bed. At 12:17 in the morning, a car pulled into the driveway. "That's Daddy! That's Daddy!" her two older children cried. Then came the rifle blast. Evers instantly knew what it was, knew "that our lives would be changed forever." The children dropped to the floor and crawled toward the safety of the bathroom, as they had been taught to do. When Evers got outside, she found her husband lying facedown on the doorstep in a pool of blood, his keys in his hand. He died a half hour later.

It was the beginning of a long-lasting nightmare, Evers opening her front door each day to see the bloodstains still visible in the concrete, running her hand across the bullet hole left in the refrigerator door, try-ing to console her children, to contain her grief and her rage. For three decades she persevered, finally bringing Medgar's killer, Bryon De La Beckwith, to justice. Today Myrlie Evers-Williams lives in Bend, Ore-gon. She is chairman of the National Association for the Advancement of Colored People (NAACP). Her eldest grandchild, Daniel Medgar Evers-Everette, is eighteen and lives in California.

Dear Danny,

When you were four days old, I walked into your parents' bedroom and you were lying there on the bed. You looked so much like Medgar! I asked everyone to leave the room, and then I just stood there and stared at you. You had your hands balled into fists, the way babies do, your arms above your head, like a prizefighter making the victory sign. In my mind, I said, "Medgar, you can't see this child. Or perhaps you can?" And I picked you up and held you and began to sob, because Medgar missed seeing his first grandchild. And then I wondered what you would have to face, a male, African-American child, in this country, in this time. What on earth would you have to face?

Many times, when you were younger, you asked me, "Grandma-ma, why would this bad man kill my grandfather when he didn't do anything to anybody except try to help?" We've told you stories about what things were like then, about the things for which your grandfather was fighting. About how we couldn't vote or run for public office, how we were denied equal education and equal access to jobs, how we were barred from the pools and the parks and the libraries and even the dressing rooms in stores, how in movie theaters we had to sit up in the balcony—the "buzzard's roost," it was called. You listen as we tell you these things, and then you shake your head, and say, "I don't see how you lived with that. I'd never put up with it. I'd never tolerate it." And I don't think your generation would, not in the manner that we did.

You are eighteen now, and not a small child anymore, though there are still things you don't know yet, things I would like to tell you, so that you will think about them as you move through your life. Life is a testing ground, Danny. I've lived through a lot, and I'm not sure there is anything I would change. I'm a human being. I have strengths and weaknesses, and I'm fortunate to be able to recognize most of my weaknesses. I work daily to strengthen those areas of my life. But one key thing I have learned is that you can't expect a perfect world, or perfect people in it. And you won't get very far if you blame other people or the world for the unfortunate things that happen in your life.

When your grandfather was killed, I was consumed with hatred to the point that my motivation for staying alive was to get even. After they took Medgar away to the hospital that night, I remember the anger—not only with his killer but with friends and neighbors who had kept me from going with him and with the police, who had harassed us day and night. I simply wanted to get a gun and mow them all down. I was very vocal about these feelings before my children. And they said to me, "Mommy, why are you saying these things? Daddy said we shouldn't hate." It brought back something that Medgar said to me not long before he was killed: "Myrlie, hatred of another human being is below you. It destroys you." So I decided to turn my hatred into the more positive force of persistence, to move on in my own life and do what I could do to keep Medgar's memory alive. From this point on, Danny, you too must take responsibility for yourself and for the things that you do with your life.

You have your grandfather's name and I know you've always felt some pressure because of that. Sometimes people have said to you: "Well, we know you're going to be just like your grandad," or "You look just like your grandad," and expectations can be a burden. I know you've felt like you had to excel in everything in order to uphold his name and not let the family down—you shouldn't be saddled with all that. I want you to know that your grandfather would be very proud of you, Daniel, for finishing high school, for accomplishing something positive. You could have dropped out. You could have become a member of a gang. You could have become addicted to drugs. There have been times when I have wondered, "Dear God, how long will he be able to be safe?" The fact that you have survived for eighteen years to become the fine young man that you are says an awful lot. There are very difficult challenges yet before you. I wonder: Will you have to be doubly or triply better than someone else in order to get a decent job? You will not have the opportunities, free of prejudice and racism, that your grandfather died for.

But no matter what happens, I don't want you to ever fall into a mode of self-pity and give up on your dreams. If you have something that you believe in strongly enough to pursue—even though all odds may appear to be against you, even though others might try to dissuade you—then you do it. Be prepared for all kinds of roadblocks being thrown in your way, and realize that it's only through these tests that we become stronger human beings and that one must persevere— just persevere. If you ever reach a point where you're satisfied with the status quo and refuse to take risks and refuse to listen to what your heart, and your mind, your intelligence, say, then you might as well stop breathing.

My own grandmother gave me some important words of wisdom that I would like to pass on to you now. "God," she said, "is like the potter. You are the clay. The potter molds the clay into the vessel he wishes it to be, and it can be very beautiful. But that pottery does not become strong, almost unbreakable, until it is placed in the fire. Only then does the real beauty, the real strength shine through." She told me that years and years ago, and I have never forgotten. Stand with your arms open to all that life has to bring to you, whether it is negative or positive, because in doing so, you will become stronger, and your journey through this planet will have real meaning.

Love,
Grandma-ma Myrlie

*Even in junior high, he had an instinct for political phrasemaking, run-
ning successfully for student council president on the campaign slogan
"Elect Ralph Reed, The Little Giant." Two decades later, Reed's Christian Coalition is a little giant of another sort: In a few short years, the
organization has changed the face of American politics, pushing family
issues center stage and helping set the agenda for the Republican party.*

*Yet Reed's political savvy and leadership ability are combined with
strong devotion to his own family. "You don't realize how much your
deepest hopes and longings are tied up in your children, but they are," he
says. Reed counts as the two most important experiences in his life his
marriage to Jo Anne, twenty-eight, and the gradual deepening of his
faith in God. The Reeds have three children: Christopher, three; Ralph
III, five; and Brittany, seven.*

Dear Brittany:

You were our "dissertation baby." Your mother and I found out she
was pregnant with you on a hot Saturday morning in July, just a few
days after we celebrated our first anniversary. I was on my way to the
library for another marathon weekend of studying. Your mother took a
home pregnancy test, then ran into the bedroom of our small apartment
with tears welling up in her eyes. She woke me up by jumping into bed,
squealing with joy. I held her as she shook in my arms like a leaf blown
loose to an autumn breeze. We were both overwhelmed. You were so
real to us, even at that early stage.

Afterwards, we spent the morning at the Georgia State archives,
struggling away on my dissertation, researching the residential patterns
of students at church-related colleges in the 1850s. It was like that
throughout the pregnancy and the first year of your life. I was a graduate student at Emory University, completing a doctorate in American
history. Your mother worked at an engineering firm in Atlanta. We
never had much money, but we had big dreams. And we had you.

I can still remember staying home with you after your mother went
back to work and balancing your little body on my lap while I tapped

"In God's eyes, the cooing of a baby weighs
more heavily than the daily uptick of the stock market."
RALPH REED

*Ralph and Jo Anne Reed with children Brittany, Ralph III,
and Christopher (in Jo Anne's arms)*

away on the computer. I was a regular "Mr. Mom," and about as well-intentioned a failure as most men at that job. Each morning, I rose at six A.M. and worked until I heard your cries from the nursery, then fed you breakfast with milk that Mom had left in the freezer. We would call your mother several times a day at her office, and you would cry heartily into the phone so she could continue to feed you. (Her immediate supervisor didn't think much of this technique, but it worked for us.)

You spent the morning playing with rattles or toying with the lace at the base of the beautiful blue quilt that draped our bed. The latter kept you occupied for hours, to my utter amazement. One day, I spent an entire morning assembling a musical rocking chair which would lull you to sleep for hours at a stretch while I slaved away at the computer a few feet away. Often, I would take a break in the afternoon and walk you in your stroller down to a nearby pond, where I read musty old history books, you gurgled peacefully in the stroller, and we fed the ducks together.

At the time, it seemed like such a struggle—writing feverishly under an approaching deadline, taking care of a new baby, waiting tables at night, and applying for fellowships and teaching jobs. Now I know those were the most precious times of our lives.

Later, when I took the job as executive director of the Christian Coalition, we packed up our few possessions and moved to Virginia Beach, Virginia, where I was born twenty-eight years earlier. Your mother worked as my secretary for a short time; we opened the mail that poured in by the bucket until after midnight; our Bible study group stuffed envelopes in our den, while we ate pizza and you played on the floor. At night, your mother and I would put you in the crib and give you your favorite stuffed animal, a little McGruff crime dog, complete with brown trench coat and cap. Years later, after you were in elementary school, your mother sent me to Toys for Tots to donate some old toys after we had cleaned out the attic. I began to unload the trunk of my car and there among the tattered and discarded contents of the Hefty bags, stuffed to overflowing, I found that old McGruff. I stood there in that parking lot feeling like a fool as tears streamed down my face. I think I had gotten more attached to that old dog than you did. We gave away everything except McGruff.

I suppose if I had one simple lesson to carry away from those days, it would be the overarching sovereignty of God in our lives, even in the mundane and seemingly unimportant. In God's eyes, the cooing of a baby weighs more heavily than the daily uptick of the stock market; fixing the broken bicycle of a child counts for more than purchasing a new luxury automobile; and helping little hands learn to tie a shoe means more in the span of eternity than writing a best-selling book. Our society delegates these duties almost exclusively to mothers, to the detriment of too many men. As you grow older, I pray you rise as high and as far as your talents can carry you. But I also hope your husband knows the joy of taking care of little ones, not only because it will be his duty in helping you, but because it will be good for him. I will always be grateful that I spent your first six months holding you in my arms, feeding you and changing you, instead of furrowing the fields of largely vain enterprises the world considers more important than our children.

I needed to learn those things, and I never could have learned them except by looking through the eyes of your vulnerability and innocence. I finally finished the dissertation when you were two years old— yes, it took that long. At the graduation ceremony, I anxiously searched the crowd for the faces of you, your mother, and your little brother. How much more all of you had come to mean to me than that piece of sheepskin!

There is a verse in the Book of Psalms that promises, "Delight yourself in the Lord, and He will give you the desires of your heart." Marrying your mother, having you and your brothers, taught me that the best desires are not those we covet and then strain to realize but, rather, His desires, which we only discover by relinquishing our wants and submitting to His will. This is how you came into our lives. Our plan was to wait until I had finished my doctorate, until I had my first teaching job in a sleepy college town somewhere in the South, before the babies began arriving. We had been advised to do so by those much wiser than we, by our parents, in-laws and such. But God had a different plan, so much richer and more textured in experience, so full of wisdom and love. Not only did you come so quickly and wonderfully, but that teaching job never arrived, and I received a call to help launch a new grassroots organization that altered not only our lives but the lives of many others.

When your mother and I were engaged, I thought we should wait a few years to get married, until I was done with graduate school (my favorite excuse for postponing just about everything) and could earn a decent living. Your mother humored me, but in the end she got her way. After the formal engagement, we visited Long Island, ostensibly for Thanksgiving but really more for my audition before the prospective in-laws. It is one of those rites of passage so excruciating and yet so unavoidable that all one can do is grin a lot, struggle to remember names, and speak in measured sentences to avoid the inevitable faux pas. We ate turkey and dressing, watched football games on television, visited New York City and went shopping, during which I did my best to remain on my best behavior. I gather I passed the audition because your mother didn't cancel the wedding.

Following the last family get-together of the weekend, your mother and I headed for the Long Island Expressway in her blue Toyota, the one with the hatchback trunk and the sporting strips down the side, which seemed oddly out of place. As we prepared to get on the New Jersey Turnpike, I nearly missed my turn and swerved back to the right in the direction of the tollbooths. The left rear tire clipped the median in the highway, causing the car to careen across four lanes, right in the path of a hail of oncoming holiday traffic, finally banging on its side, flipping back upright and coming to rest in a haze of blue smoke and gravel on the side of the road. I had no control of the car from the moment we jumped the median until we stopped. Yet when I got out of the car, expecting to see the entire side of the vehicle torn away, there was not a scratch on the paint.

There we sat with two blown tires, waiting for a tow truck, two frightened people who had been nearly killed just months before their wedding day. Why had our lives been spared? To that we had no real answer, except that maybe God had a purpose for our lives for which we had been spared. From that moment on, we began to believe that we were a subplot in a much larger drama, part of something much bigger than ourselves, that our marriage had a purpose beyond our own personal fulfillment. So remember two things: First, after you purchase your first car don't let your boyfriend behind the wheel. Second, always remember that you were a blessing to us, but most of all the product of a relationship whose end was not in itself, but in bringing healing to a bruised and hurting world beyond the walls of our love.

I once worked for a man who had a sign on the wall of his office that read, "Dream dreams so big that they are sure to fail unless God intervenes." Good advice, all. Dream as big as you can, and then some. Who knows? It might actually happen. Finally, always remember the lesson you taught us: While working in a frenzy to realize those dreams, be sure to smell the flowers along the way.

Love,
Dad

U.S. Army Captain Thomas C. Metsker died on November 14, 1965, at Ia Drang Valley, a casualty of the first major battle of the Vietnam War. His daughter, Karen, was seventeen months old. She was left with a box of his possessions, stored by her mother in the basement, with recurrent nightmares, with a thousand unanswered questions and an unstoppable longing for the father she never knew.

In 1987, she married Scott Rudel, and found in him a man who understood. The couple have three children—Abigail, six, Alison, eight, and Thomas Alexander, four. They live in Ipswich, Massachusetts, in a white clapboard house with blue shutters, a trellis in the garden. Thomas, their youngest child, is named for his grandfather.

Dear Ali, Abi and Lex,

If the notion that your mom is different from other people has not yet occurred to you, someday it will. It took me years to come to terms with the idea that I would never fit the mainstream mold.

The path my life has taken was decided by a single bullet in a little country in Southeast Asia known as Vietnam. On the first day of the first "Search-and-Destroy" mission, in a battle in the Ia Drang Valley, November 1965, my father, your grandpa, was wounded in the shoulder as he tried to rally other soldiers to help a platoon in distress. He made his way back to the landing zone, X-Ray, where he boarded a helicopter and waited to be evacuated. Another man, more severely wounded, was being lifted in on a poncho—I've had nightmares about that man for years. My father got out to help load him into the helicopter. That was when the fatal bullet hit.

None of it makes any more sense to me now than it did when I was growing up. I have spent countless hours talking to my dad, asking him questions which others have tried to settle for me, knowing that only his answers would do. Why did he get off that helicopter? How could he shoot another person? Why did he go to Vietnam? Why did he get married, knowing that the wife he loved could so easily be widowed? Why did he have me, knowing that I could so easily be left fatherless?

"Loss is an inevitable part of life. When it is unexpected or early it leaves emotional scars which can fade, but will never disappear."
KAREN RUDEL

Karen Rudel with children Lex, Alison (front left), and Abigail

How could he, as a son, as a brother, take such a risk? I still desperately want the answers to these questions. They will never come.

I want those answers for you, too. For most of my life I have had the strangest sensation, of not really knowing half of myself. I wonder what my father's voice sounded like, how he laughed, how he moved. Am I the same as I would have been if he had lived? Are you?

As I watch you grow, I wish you could have known your grandpa and that wish is tainted by the nagging question of whether he and I would have agreed on a very basic philosophical level. Some of the things he stood for go against everything I believe in. But if he had raised me, I would have grown up on military bases. And perhaps I, too, would have seen military force and killing other human beings as a solution to disagreements between governments.

I remember the time before my mother, Kate, remarried. We had moved back to southern Indiana so she could be near her family, a twenty-four-year-old widow with a seventeen-month-old daughter. I can't begin to imagine the struggle she must have faced every day as she put me in day care, taught school, worked on her master's degree and raised me in that tiny white house with black shutters on Chandler Street.

A year after she married Poppins, your Uncle Doug was born. Then came Aunt Susie. Your Aunt Julie and Uncle Mike were children from his first marriage, and they were with us a lot. Kate was busy with babies, a situation I only understood fully after I had you. I felt separate and alone. I wished for a full-blooded sibling, someone who could understand the vacant space within me, who could know the longing for my father's touch and empathize with my insatiable longing.

I never knew anyone else who lost his dad in Vietnam. In fact, I was the only person I knew who didn't have both biological parents at home. Because Poppins adopted me, few people knew that I wasn't really his child, but I felt that I never fit in, at home or among my peers.

Inside, I was feeling worse and worse. The older I got, the more questions I had. No one talked about my dad. I don't know if it was because it made Poppins uncomfortable or because it made my mom sad. So I left the questions unasked.

Sometimes, I would sneak down to the basement and go through the few things of my dad's that my mom had saved. I would sit in that basement and cry as I picked up one thing after another, each one, to me, my dad. A scrapbook with some photos and old newspaper clippings about his death, the teddy bear he and Mom had given me when I was a baby, the flag folded up in a triangle which had been draped over his coffin during the funeral at Arlington Cemetery, a handful of medals, including a Purple Heart. There was also a Father's Day card my mother had sent him from me. On the inside, it said, "'cause I'll always be Daddy's little girl."

By sixth grade, my unhappiness was apparent to others. My teacher, Mr. Lloyd, may have been the first with the courage to voice his concern. But I saw it as a confrontation. He kept me after class and asked, "Karen, why don't you smile?" How could I explain to him the empty feeling I had? How could I talk about my overwhelming sense of loss, the feeling that I didn't fit in anywhere? He asked me the question over and over again, and I cried and refused to answer. When he finally released me, my classmates laughed at me because they saw I had been crying.

That may have been the point at which I began to build walls—emotional strongholds, really—to protect myself from the pain of loss, humiliation and separation. The walls got higher and thicker as I got older, and I shut out more and more painful feelings. I suppose some of it was normal adolescent growing pains. But I felt even more helpless not being able to turn to my daddy for help.

I'm sure I built up the image of my dad to superhero proportions. It's improper to speak ill of the dead, so the little I heard about him was how wonderful he was and what a good athlete, what a good sense of humor he had. I knew in my heart he would have loved me more than anything in the world, and backed me whether I was right or wrong.

I wish you could understand the struggle I went through to find your father, my husband. I went out with a lot of jerks and some nice guys, too, but no one met the criteria I had set up until I met your dad. My ideal husband had to be intelligent, had to question authority and be unable to be drafted into the military. He also had to have the potential to be a wonderful father. By my definition, this meant he needed to change diapers, read stories, be active in sports without watching them on TV constantly, and love his children. Your dad is all these things and more. He is my gift to you. He is as close as I can come to the assurance that you will never have to struggle through the emotional turmoil I have.

I finally met the men who fought with my dad in that battle almost thirty years ago. On the twenty-fifth anniversary of Ia Drang, we went to Washington for a reunion. I was terrified to meet these men. I envisioned them as stereotypical movie-type Vietnam veterans: macho, chest-beating killers, pro-war types. As a pacifist, I was afraid I would be unwelcome, and would have nothing in common with them. To my complete and utter surprise, I walked into a room full of uncles. My surrogate family embraced me and we all cried. We knew that it was only by the luck of the draw that their children had not been left fatherless as I had been.

The man my dad helped load into the helicopter survived. I wrote to him asking to meet him, although I didn't know why. Without hesitation, Ray LeFebvre left his home, full of family members in town for his daughter's wedding, to come to see me. His daughter, I think, is about my age. My nightmares stopped. For this I will always be grateful, to both him and his daughter.

That week I outlived my dad. It was a turning point for me. Facing those men helped start a healing process which I presume will not end in my lifetime. It tore down walls nearly two decades old, and strengthened my pacifist beliefs—no one should have to go through what those men have gone through, what I have gone through.

I sometimes worry that I was the one to bring you into this difficult world. But I thank you for letting me be your Mommy and for your unconditional love. I hope I can guide you, support you, and keep you from making my many mistakes.

I feel really sad when I think of the thousands of other children who have lost parents at an early age. But loss is an inevitable part of life. When it is unexpected or early, it leaves emotional scars. The scars can fade, but they will never disappear.

I love you unconditionally and forever.
Mommy

"In Vietnam, your father and I discovered
the cement that binds men together."
JAMES MARTIN DAVIS

James Martin Davis

*Not long after Jim Davis arrived in Vietnam, a veteran sergeant offered
the following advice: "If you want to stay alive, remember three things.
Do what you're told. Look out for each other. And keep your ass in the
grass with everybody else." By the time Davis returned from active duty
a year later, he understood just how basic and profound a lesson it was.
The war, Davis says, taught him to endure, to draw strength and
courage from deep inside himself, to put the lives of others above his own.
He knew that if he survived, "life would never be so hard again."*

*Yet like many other veterans, Jim Davis has never completely left
Vietnam behind. Now a prominent lawyer in Omaha, Nebraska, he
writes and talks about his experiences in the war in part to deal with the
pain and loss. "I miss those guys," he says. "I miss that time in my life.
It's a bond that can never be dissolved." Most of all, Davis misses his
friend and fellow soldier, Jerry Wilder, who died in 1983. Wilder's children are now grown, living on the East Coast. Says Davis: "I want
them to know about their dad. Every child has that right."*

Dear Kathy, Kimberly, Jennifer, and Jerilyn.

I am not sure you will remember me, but a long time ago when you
were little children, I met you at your father's funeral. Since you were all
so small, you probably remember very little about that day and who was
there. But your father was as close to me as a brother, and it is a day that
I will never forget.

A few months ago, I received a telephone call from your mother. She
said that Jerry's little girls were now grown women, asking about the
father they never knew and his activities in Vietnam. She asked me if I
could write and tell you about his military service and about the time we
spent together as soldiers.

I want you to know that I am delighted to be able to do so. I served
in Vietnam from June of 1969 to June of 1970 and, for the last eleven
months of my tour, I served with your father. He was one of the closest
friends I ever had. He was a decent, courageous, fun-loving gentleman
soldier, and even after all these years I think of him often.

Your father and I, along with a number of other handpicked soldiers, served in a special combat unit based out of An Khe in the Central Highlands. Most of our missions were classified. As part of our primary duties, we undertook patrols, planting electronic detection and eaves-dropping devices along jungle trails, on enemy avenues of approach, and near enemy base camps. The sensors detected enemy footsteps, body heat, metal weapons, and voices. Our job was to locate and then penetrate promising areas, to implant the devices, and then to get out of the area without being detected ourselves. It was very dangerous work.

Although I had a lot of friends in Vietnam, none was closer to me than your father. I want you to know that I loved and respected him as only one combat soldier can love and respect another. I miss him very much. Even after all this time, it is hard for me to accept that he is gone. I can still picture his face and his smile. It is a dirty and a sweaty face, with a big, impish grin hiding the fear. I remember the insults we traded and the cigarettes we shared, the things we did. But most of all, I re-member how he clung to the thought of his family and to the promise of tomorrow. Your father made me laugh and he made me proud, and when he died, a part of me died with him. He was just about the most thoroughly decent man that I have ever known.

Vietnam was an important experience for your father and me, and for many of us who fought there. We were spoiled young kids—Baby Boomers—when we went to war, but Vietnam changed us. Vietnam was hard: It meant mud and marshes, dirt and dust, machetes and monsoons. We suffered from the stings of fire ants, the relentless nuisance of the leeches, our arms and legs burning with cuts and scratches. Through these experiences we came to recognize how resilient we humans really are, because we learned to live with these things every day and we endured.

Together, Jerry and I recognized that we were becoming stronger, both mentally and physically, than we had ever been before. Deep in-side ourselves, we discovered a confidence we had never known. But most of all, we discovered a pride in each other and in our team that we never knew could exist. We lost our selfishness and no matter how hard things became, it was this new feeling of empathy, devotion, loyalty, and enthusiasm that kept us going. In Vietnam, your father and I discovered the cement that binds men together.

In real life, soldiers don't fight for their country so much as they fight for each other. Our first commandment had been to look after your buddy, because he is looking out for you. Our rule was to perish if we must, but to save our buddy first.

Your father and I learned things about ourselves that no classroom could ever teach. We learned in combat that the measure of a man has nothing to do with how much money he has, or where he comes from, or the color of his skin. It is governed by a simple equation: When it comes down to a situation involving life and death, will those around him be able to trust him with their lives? Your father filled that equation perfectly. I cannot tell you how many times—whether in the field, on patrol, standing guard, or in countless other situations—I put my life in his hands. A soldier's language is coarse and profane because war is coarse and profane. Yet despite the crudeness of our language, our simple phrases said so much. We used to say to other soldiers that if they wanted to go on patrol with us, they had to have their "shit together." No other soldier I knew had his "shit together" like Jerry Wilder.

Back home, people safe from the war in distance and time debated whether it was wrong or right. We never had time to debate the war, we only had time to fight it. Still, your father and I were both college graduates, and it was something on our minds every day. For all their horror, wars are stories of people at their best as well as at their worst. Our soldiers saved lives as well as took them. They built hospitals, orphanages, and schools. They fed the hungry, tended the sick, clothed the naked, and ministered to the poor.

Your father was one of those special soldiers. When we got passes, most guys would go into town, hanging out at the bars or the cathouses. Jerry never did that. We would find him later at the Catholic church school and orphanage on Highway 19 in An Khe. He was with the priests, visiting the kids because he really loved kids and he knew he could help.

In November 1969, your father was awarded a Bronze Star for a mission around a rubber plantation near Ban Mi Thuot. This action resulted in the discovery of an enemy base camp area, and the death of three enemy soldiers. He was also awarded the air medal for missions dropping sensors from helicopters in areas inaccessible to our troops, and for his combat assaults by chopper into enemy territory.

Up until the time I left Vietnam, I counted on your dad for everything. I remember one night, in late April 1970, when I had only a few weeks to go before I rotated home, I was awakened and told to report to the command trailer. Once inside, I saw several officers around a map. They advised me that I would be taking a mission into Base 442, in advance of a 4th Division operation. After I left the trailer, the impact of what I had just been told hit me with full force. I couldn't believe it. I had come this far and just when I started to believe I was going to make it home, I was being sent into Cambodia.

When I got back to our hooch, your father was still awake, and I asked him to come outside. Of all the soldiers in our unit, I knew I could count on him the most, so I told him what was in store for me. I wrote my parents' name and address on a piece of paper, and I gave it to your father. He took that piece of paper from me, and tightly squeezed my hand with both of his. Without my saying a word, he instinctively knew what I was thinking and what to do. "Jim, don't worry about a thing," he said. "I'll take care of everything." With those simple words, my mind was cleared. If anything happened to me, I knew that your father would handle it.

Thankfully, I survived our invasion of Cambodia, and in June 1970, I left Vietnam and your father behind. A month later, he returned to the States as well, but I never saw him again. We had always planned how we were going to get together, how we were going to do things—you know, we thought we had all the time in the world.

Jerry was never the same after he got back from Vietnam. He was sick a lot, the result of Agent Orange. He had spent thirty days monitoring sensing devices on a mountain which had been completely defoliated by the chemical. When he had his heart attack, I wanted to come and see him, but he wanted me to wait until after the transplant. Sadly, he didn't survive the surgery. I've kicked myself a million times for not coming anyway.

Your father was buried with full military honors, and just as in Vietnam, I was at his side. I remember seeing you there, four little girls, two sets of twins—how darling you looked. When they lowered his coffin, each of you, one at a time, placed a red rose on top of the casket. At the cemetery, I thought of the war and how long it had been over, and how unfair it had been. Vietnam asked so little from so many, but asked so much from you few. Here was a family that had been robbed of it all— lost laughter, lost innocence, lost youth, and lost dreams. Yet, despite your loss, you all stood tall and remained proud. That is the way you should always remain. Jerry Wilder was a hell of a soldier, and a hell of a friend. Being there that day was the toughest duty I had as a soldier.

I want each of you always to remember that for me, serving with your father was a privilege I never deserved, and from his example I learned so much about life and even more about living. Your father is special to me, and a little piece of him will always be inside of me.

Despite the fact that he is gone, he and I will forever be joined at the soul.

Your father and I went to war and we shared it together, the same sights and sounds, the same feelings and fears, the same tastes and smells. We shared love and respect, loyalty and trust, and we shared the unspoken promise always to look after each other. This letter is to fulfill in part that unspoken promise.

Sincerely,
Jim Davis

"For your father, there were no hard choices in life.
Once he committed to something, the way was clear."
CARMEN GORDON

Carmen Gordon with children Brittany and Ian

All around Carmen Gordon's house in Southern Pines, North Carolina, are pictures of her late husband. A bedroom holds his medals, his uniforms, the books he read. "I tried to save everything that might give the kids an idea of what their dad was like," she says. On October 3, 1993, Master Sergeant Gary Gordon was fatally shot in Mogadishu, Somalia, while trying to rescue a wounded helicopter pilot. He was awarded the Medal of Honor in 1994. In a letter Gordon left for his wife, he told her to never look back. Don't dwell on something you can't change, he said.

Brittany, five, and Ian, eight, remember their father vividly, speak about him often. Their mother's hopes for their future are these: That they will be strong and kind, that they will follow through. Her only fear is of losing her children. "When I look in their eyes, I see Gary's strength in them, and his spirit," she says. "They give me the strength to carry on."

Dear Ian and Brittany,

I hope that in the final moments of your father's life, his last thoughts were not of us. As he lay dying, I wanted him to think only of the mission to which he pledged himself. As you grow older, if I can show you the love and responsibility he felt for his family, you will understand my feelings. I did not want him to think of me, or of you, because I did not want his heart to break.

Children were meant to have someone responsible for them. No father ever took that more seriously than your dad. Responsibility was a natural part of him, an easy path to follow. Each day after work his truck pulled into our driveway. I watched the two of you run to him, feet pounding across the painted boards of our porch, yelling, "Daddy!" Every day, I saw his face when he saw you. You were the center of his life.

Ian, when you turned one year old, your father was beside himself with excitement, baking you a cake in the shape of a train. The month before he died, Brittany, he sent you a handmade birthday card from Somalia. But your father had two families. One was us, and the other was his comrades. He was true to both.

He loved his job. Quiet and serious adventure filled some part of him I could never fully know. After his death, one of his comrades told me that on a foreign mission, your dad led his men across a snow-covered ridge that began to collapse. Racing across a yawning crevasse to safety, he grinned wildly and yelled, "Wasn't that great?"

You will hear many times about how your father died. You will read what the president of the United States said when he awarded the Medal of Honor: "Gary Gordon . . . died in the most courageous and selfless way any human being can act." But you may still ask why. You may ask how he could have been devoted to two families so equally, dying for one but leaving the other.

For your father, there were no hard choices in life. Once he committed to something, the way was clear. He chose to be a husband and father, and never wavered in those roles. He chose the military, and "I shall not fail those with whom I serve" became his simple religion. When his other family needed him, he did not hesitate, as he would not have hesitated for us. It may not have been the best thing for us, but it was the right thing for your dad.

There are times now when that image of him coming home comes back to me. I see him scoop you up, Ian, and see you, Brittany, bury your head in his chest. I dread the day when you stop talking and asking about him, when he seems so long ago. So now I must take responsibility for keeping his life entwined with yours. It is a responsibility I never wanted.

But I know what your father would say. "Nothing you can do about it, Carmen. Just keep going." Those times when the crying came, as I stood at the kitchen counter, were never long enough. You came in the front door, Brittany, saying, "Mommy, you sad? You miss Daddy?" You reminded me I had to keep going.

The ceremonies honoring your dad were hard. When they put his photo in the Hall of Heroes at the Pentagon, I thought, Can this be all that is left, a picture? Then General Sullivan read from the letter General Sherman wrote to General Grant after the Civil War, words so tender that we all broke down: "Throughout the war, you were always in my mind, I always knew if I were in trouble and you were still alive you would come to my assistance."

One night before either of you were born, your dad and I had a funny little talk about dying. I teased that I would not know where to bury him. Very quietly, he said, "Up home. In my uniform." Your dad never liked to wear a uniform. And "up home," Maine, was so far away from us.

Only after he was laid to rest in a tiny flag-filled graveyard in Lincoln, Maine, did I understand. His parents, burying their only son, could come tomorrow and the day after that. You and I would not have to pass his grave on the way to the grocery store, to Little League games, to ballet recitals. Our lives would go on. And to the men he loved and died for, the uniform was a silent salute, a final repeat of his vows. Once again, he had taken care of all of us.

On a spring afternoon, a soldier from your dad's unit brought me the things from his military locker. At the bottom of a cardboard box, beneath his boots, I found a letter. Written on a small, ruled tablet, it was his voice, quiet but confident in the words he wanted us to have if something should happen to him. I'll save it for you, but so much of him is already inside you both. Let it grow with you. Choose your own responsibilities in life but always, always follow your heart. Your dad will be watching over you, just as he always did.

Love,
Mom

"There is something about saying words aloud that strengthens our relationship with them."
RABBI JAY ROSENBAUM

Jay Rosenbaum and son David

Rabbi Rosenbaum picks up his tallit, beginning the morning service, intoning the lines of the psalm as he has done countless times before: "Let all my being praise the Lord who is clothed in splendor and majesty, wrapped in light as in a garment, unfolding the heavens like a curtain." He kisses the prayer shawl, wraps it around himself, his actions echoing the words of the prayer. The ritual is one of Rosenbaum's favorites, a "poetic, powerful image with which to start the day," a brief moment that sets a spiritual rhythm, keeping the miracle of the ordinary before him as he moves through the crowded hours of meetings, services, hospital visits, bar mitzvahs, weddings, funerals.

As the leader of Congregation Beth Israel in Worcester, Massachusetts, Rosenbaum strives to make Judaism come alive in a time of soul-searching, when many Jews are returning to religious observance, but many more have left God behind. As a youth, the rabbi, too, went through a crisis of faith, deciding finally at twenty-five to enter the rabbinate. Much of his inspiration came from his father, also a rabbi, who died in 1978 "He never asked me to follow him, but I spent my entire life watching him. He was and is a tremendous model," Rosenbaum says. His son, David, is ten.

Dear David:

On the eighth day of your life, when you entered into the Covenant of Abraham, I spoke of the significance of your name. I called you *n'im zmirot yisrael,* "sweet singer of Israel," after your biblical namesake. Your voice was already imprinted indelibly on our hearts. The words would come later, of course. But already there was a sweet tone that was distinctly yours. Our happiness was indescribable.

At that moment, I was not thinking of what I wished to pass on to you. I was far too caught up in keeping you warm in the cold December winter, feeding you late into the night. But now, ten years have passed, and I have had more time to collect my thoughts.

You have often asked me to tell you about my father, your Zaydie. A picture of him is on your desk. They say a picture tells more than words—I am not so sure. It is my father's voice that I remember.

I wish you could have heard it as I did. It was both gentle and authoritative. It conveyed affection and, when necessary, discipline. How we dreaded his change of tone. We used to joke that when my sisters and I were little, all my father had to do was lower his voice and draw out the word *no*, and we would burst into tears.

My father's voice also inspired a lot of family teasing. He could not carry a tune very well, but he never believed us when we gave him a hard time about it on Shabbat. Despite this "handicap," my dad managed to work his way through college by chanting the Torah readings on weekends. Whatever they paid him wasn't enough. I loved to listen to him read. He read with style and passion, the way a Shakespearean actor recites a great part (he was an actor in college, you know). And like any good actor, he made the words his own. Yet his voice was also the voice of our tradition, the voice of Abraham and Moses, and at times it seemed to me, even the gentle voice of God.

When I was eleven years old, my father began to teach me to read the Torah. It was a gift that would last a lifetime and would link me with him forever. The other day when you asked me what Torah portion you would read on your Bar Mitzvah day, I answered you playfully by singing the opening line with feeling: *"Bereshi-it bara Elohim, et ha-shamayim v'et haaretz—In the beginning God created the heaven and the earth."* It was one of the first readings I learned as a child.

My father taught me to love the words of the Tanakh the way a musician loves great music. When I was a child, I participated in Bible contests in school. We called them *chidon hatanach*. The questions tested us on nuances of the text that few people would notice on a first reading. To this day, if someone were to wake me in the middle of the night and say the name Ehud ben Gera, I would respond without a moment's hesitation *"Ish iteir yad yemino—A man who didn't use his right hand,"* even though I learned this text over thirty years ago.

Memorizing the words of great literature has become something of a lost art, but one worth recapturing. When I was in grade school, I had a teacher who made us memorize famous passages from the book of Isaiah. It seemed pointless at the time, but now I'm glad I did it. There is something about saying the words aloud that strengthens our relationship with them.

There is a Hasidic custom of reading aloud every day the psalm that corresponds to the year of our birth. For me now, it is the 45th Psalm. The idea is that if we say the words daily, knowing they are "ours," after a while they begin to take on a very personal meaning. There is a line in this psalm that always makes me smile sheepishly: *"Chagor charbecha al yarech gibor*—Gird your sword on your hip, mighty one." The line was written in praise of a great Jewish king riding gloriously into battle. But when I recite it, I like to imagine it is directed at me, encouraging me in my battles as I greet the new day. I feel ever so slightly guilty at this conceit, but after all, it is "my" psalm, so I'm allowed a flight of fancy.

As you know, David, my relationship with Judaism was not always a smooth ride. But often when I wandered it was this feeling for the Hebrew language instilled in me when I was very young that brought me back. When I was twenty-two, I went to Israel as a volunteer for Sherut Laam ("Service to the People"). It was a time when my connection to religious life was shaky.

There were eleven Americans in my group and I was the only one fluent in Hebrew. Something possessed me to share my enthusiasm for the language of the Tanakh with my friends. I would read whole passages aloud on the bus, in the original Hebrew so they would get the full flavor. To this day I'm not sure why they let me get away with this, though, of course, they didn't have the option of getting off the bus.

When we are young, David, we go through a period when we struggle so hard to define what is unique about ourselves. Often we feel that we have to differentiate ourselves from everything that came before us, especially our parents. It is part of growing up.

Remember the fight we had about your baseball schedule? Half your minor league games you missed because they were on Shabbat. You were disappointed, but accepting. But when you found out that one of the few Monday games fell on Shavuot, you lost it. I took you out to Friendly's, but for a while in the car, you were so upset with me you refused to talk. When you finally did speak, your angry words had a familiar ring: "If you weren't a rabbi, I'd be able to play." "These are your commitments, not mine," you told me in so many words. Had I not said the same things to my father?

After what seemed an endless ride, we arrived at Friendly's and things cooled down a bit. And when it came time to order, you said to me, "Dad, do you have an extra *kippah*—a yarmulke? I left mine at home." I was so relieved.

It has taken me my whole life to figure out how to remain true to myself and connected to my past at the same time. I used to think that self-expression was about what was inside of me. Now I realize it is about listening, too. Of what use is it to pour out my own soul if I have no sense of whether what touches me will find a responsive chord in the heart of my friend? To sing my own song, I must learn his as well.

David, you are sensitive to the way words are spoken. I have seen you react swiftly to a slight change in tone, question me about an edge in my voice. Listen carefully, and you will hear in the words of our ancestors human beings working out the most complicated emotions, human beings working out the meaning of their lives, and God and Man struggling with each other.

Did you think you'd get by without a lesson? Here, listen to this one: "*Ma rabu maasecha hashem, kulam b'chochmah asita*—How great are your words O Lord, in wisdom you have made them all!" What intensity! The poet who wrote these words was simply thrilled to be alive. I find if I listen carefully enough to the tone of excitement in his voice, I can locate that spot within myself that feels the same way.

They say that passion and humor don't mix, but they did in my father. He was not afraid to laugh, even about the things he held most sacred. On Shabbat afternoons, we used to walk to synagogue together. I used to take an apple for the road, but for some reason this struck him as unmannered. So tongue in cheek, he used to quote me rabbinic chapter and verse: "*Haochel bashuk domeh l'kelev*—He who eats in the marketplace resembles a dog." Then he would play around with the words so that they translated "He who eats a dog resembles a marketplace." This went on every Saturday. Eventually, I would take the apple just so we could play this little game. Once again, the words of our tradition were a bond between us.

When my dad was dying, I visited him in the hospital every day. I was living in New York at the time and I was glad to be close by. I'm not sure how it began, but I started reading poetry to him. Mostly, I read from the great nationalist poet Hayim Nachman Bialik. Sometimes Bialik wrote, with great empathy, of God abandoned by his people, like a mother bird whose children have flown away. At other times, he railed at God for being silent in the face of our suffering, for not protecting Israel. Always, the poet's voice is full of feeling, a sensitive, caring voice.

My father took great comfort from hearing me read Bialik's poetry aloud. The truth is, he was getting weaker, and many times after a few minutes of reading, he began to doze off. I would stop, thinking he wanted to rest. But he would encourage me to continue. It didn't seem to matter whether he could concentrate enough to understand the poetry. He liked hearing the sound of the Hebrew words. I think he could hear in my voice, as I read, what I had heard in his voice so many times before.

David, you are pretty intense yourself. How often have I caught you lying in bed awake at night, thinking. So many questions you have. I hope I can show respect for yours, as my father did for mine. I wish you could have known your Zaydie personally. You would have liked each other a lot.

You are young now, with, God willing, a full and rich life ahead of you. Is it only chance that the most sensitive instruments of your body are your ears? Use this gift to your advantage. Make the effort to hear the voices of those who came before you. Become a passionate listener, and your own words will emerge from your heart with the force of generations. Always remember that you have your own special message to deliver. And don't be afraid to say it with feeling.

I have faith in you, you know I do. Sing sweetly, my son. You always have.

Love,
Dad

"Your home is the one place
that will love you unconditionally."
BRADLEY JENSEN

Bradley Jensen

At sixteen, Brad Jensen packed a suitcase and ran to Las Vegas, then to San Francisco, where there were other kids like him, estranged from their families, living in shelters or group homes, hanging out on the streets. He is seventeen now, and has discovered that living on his own is not so easy—last fall, he returned home to his family. He wants to be a singer, wants to sing in Broadway musicals. "I'm realizing that I'm responsible for everything I do," he says, "that I have to respect people, I have to respect their interests. But I also have to be myself." Brad's niece, Miranda, is three years old and lives with her parents in Utah, where Brad grew up. "She has a really great living situation," he says. "I wrote her this letter for when she's older, to let her know not to take it for granted."

To My Dearest Miranda:

As you grow up in a world of shelter and comfort, you will be confronted with many trials. I hope that one of those is not having to question what "home" means to you. And since I am so confronted at this time in my life, I would like to tell you my understanding of home, with the hope that it will give you comprehension in your world of love.

Other people say that I am "homeless." They confuse this phrase with what I refer to as "houseless." After all, as the cliché goes, a house is not a home. Going from small town to big city, I realize that I will never be homeless.

Home is a sense of familiarity and bonding to a place, with love. But love does not have to exist alone. Other emotions may enter. They may hold you to that place. The main idea is the understanding between you and your environment. For I believe that the environment has a spirit, and that its spirit is only what you put into it. The longer you are together the more you grow.

Your home is the one place that will love you unconditionally. But do not confuse it with the people who exist there. For it may be your home, but not theirs. Hopefully, economic stability will be yours all your life, but if it is not, remember that you will always have a home. Money is very shallow and temporary. Choose your place carefully, and thrive.

Love Always,
Bradley

For a long time, Lynda Owens thought of herself "as just a little old no-
body." Even though she was raising four children on her own, giving
them the self-discipline and fortitude to surmount urban poverty, to get
an education and forge successful lives. Even though she took in more
children, troubled kids whose parents were in jail or on drugs, and turned
their lives around. Not until she won Norman Vincent Peale's America's
Award in 1990 did it really sink in that she was making a significant
difference in the world.

Today, Owens is training for the ministry in Richmond, Virginia—
a calling the late Dr. Peale encouraged her to pursue. She also serves as
executive director of the Carver Promise, a program providing mentoring
to at-risk children in public housing developments, and she works with
the juvenile justice system. Her daughter, LaTisha, graduated from the
College of William and Mary, and is in law school at the University of
Texas.

My Dearest Daughter:

What a beautiful young lady you have become—someone with brains, personality, education, and most of all, love. LaTisha, I never had the luxury of love. I spent my entire life trying to be loved and looking for it in so many of the wrong places. I want to tell you how my life was affected by not having it.

I made many decisions with the hope of receiving love in return. My relationships with friends, and even with the men who gave life to my children, were all loveless.

At a very early age, I knew that my grandparents loved me enough to care for me, to nurture me, and to provide a spiritual foundation. But they did not teach me to understand how to handle death. I was eleven years old when they died, within months of each other. It was the worst experience of my life. I was devastated. I felt betrayed and rejected. They were the only family I knew. I lived with them because my mother was not able to take care of me, and even though my father was their son, I didn't see him very often.

"Always demand respect, but know that it is
something that is earned."
LYNDA OWENS

Lynda Owens with daughter LaTisha

When my grandparents died, I quickly turned the love they had given me into hate. I was angry at them for dying and leaving me alone. I hated myself as well. I had to move to Richmond to live with my mother. Once, I was sexually abused by a friend of the family. I told my mother about it, but she believed her boyfriend when he said he didn't do it. With my grandparents gone, my world had turned upside down. I thought that by having a child I would get the independence and love I needed. But I should have stayed in school. I should have looked for a husband who could provide a nurturing, stable home for me and my children. Instead, I chose a path that led to being a single mom. I had to work all the time, and I had to compromise in raising my children. Had I not been so selfish, I might have given you a better life. I apologize for not loving myself enough to give you all the things you needed to grow, for not making better decisions, and for not selecting partners for the right reasons.

Yet I did learn from my experiences. When you graduated from high school, I took stock of my own life and I began to work to gain a better appreciation of myself. I remembered the spiritual foundation my grandparents had given me and I started to build on that. Now I dedicate my time to helping people who do not have love in their lives. I like working with young people—pregnant teenagers especially—trying to help and to redirect them.

My own childhood was interrupted: I became a mom at sixteen. I have tried always to be honest with you, LaTisha, because I would hate for you to experience what I did. I want my children to plan for the future and to make responsible decisions. You've never given me a minute of trouble and you never rejected my parenting directives. Maybe you're successful enough now that you don't need my advice anymore. But there are still a few things I want to reinforce in your mind:

Always make decisions you can live with. If you decide to be a failure, the choice was yours. Don't blame racism, society, or anyone else. If you decide to be a success, don't let others claim responsibility for what you achieved on your own, but credit those who helped you along the way. Always demand respect, but know that it is something that is earned. Don't let a man determine the respect you receive. Retain your dignity: Ignore characterizations that demean you. You realized at a very young age that knowledge is power. So remember that regardless of one's race, creed, or color, knowledge is the common denominator that balances everything.

You may not know this, but when I was a little girl I wanted to be a lawyer when I grew up. Now you are in law school. As the daughter of a teenage mom, people predicted you would end up getting pregnant as a teenager, too. They expected you to be a school dropout, to end up as a resident of a public housing project, having children one after another. You grew up in a community that has so many negatives and so much encouragement to fail. There were a lot of opportunities to become a nobody, and a lot of excuses to rationalize that decision. But you chose not to go in that direction. You chose to listen, instead. To be respectable. I'm proud of you, LaTisha, and I thank you for loving me and allowing me to love you unconditionally.

Love always,
Your Mom

*Four days passed before rescuers located twenty-three-year-old Frankie
Merrell's body in the wreckage of the Alfred P. Murrah Federal Building
in Oklahoma City, days during which her mother and stepfather,
Marsha and Tom Kight, waited, "hoping for the best but preparing for
the worst." In the time since the April 1995 bombing, the Kights have
begun slowly to piece together their lives, in part by helping others.
Among other things, Marsha is working to establish a resource center for
victims' families. Frankie's daughter, Morgan, is three.*

Dear Morgan:

Somewhere I once read: "Life sees you coming. She lies in wait for
you. She cannot but hurt you." If I could somehow keep pain from you,
it would be life itself that I would be keeping out.

Pain is part of life, as is joy. You cannot go over it. You cannot go
around it. You must go through it. But we will always be here to love and
support you through whatever life may bring you.

I want you to know what a wonderful person your mother was, and
about the values with which she chose to live her life. When your
mother was in elementary school at Lake Park in Oklahoma City, they
had a special care center for handicapped students. Because her grandmother was an amputee, your mother learned to see only the qualities a
person has inside, and not to care about outward appearances. She took
time and special interest in these children. They were her friends.

She was loving and giving, always thinking of others first. The day
you were born was the happiest day of her life. After she returned to
work, she spent all her spare time with you. She, too, experienced pain
with the death of her father in 1994. She had just begun to pull her life
back together when evil took her away from us all. Now I will try to tell
you what happened on April 19, 1995, the day your mother became an
angel.

The day before, you, your mother, and Poo-Pah all went to dinner
and to a movie. I had a class that night—I'd started back to college not
long before. When I got home from class, you were sound asleep on

"Your mom's love will always be with you.
Love does not die, people do."
MARSHA KIGHT

Tom and Marsha Kight with granddaughter Morgan

Poo-Pah's chest, and your mom had already gone home. Before she left, she gave you and Poo-Pah a big hug and kiss and said, "I love you." I spoke with your mother briefly late that night. We made plans for lunch the next day. We were to meet her at 10:50 A.M. I told her that I loved her and was looking forward to seeing her the next day. Her last words to me were: "I love you, Mom. Good night."

Several times before, you and I had met your mom for lunch. We would arrive early and ride the elevator to the third floor of the Federal Building, go through some doors, then down a hallway to the tellers' area. Her window was always adorned with your pictures. A big smile would cross her face and her eyes would light up when she saw you come through the door.

That morning, I took my shower while you were still sleeping. I had just stepped out of the shower when I heard a terrible explosion. From the sound, I thought a gas line had ruptured down the street at a construction site. I threw on my robe and rushed outside. Everything appeared normal. A woman came walking down the street and I asked if she knew what had happened. She said she'd heard the explosion was downtown, and continued with her walk.

I ran back into the house, and called Poo-Pah's office, to ask if he knew anything. He said no, but told me to turn on the TV and call him back if I heard anything. Standing near the phone, I picked up the remote and turned on the television. Instantly, I saw the building where your mother worked: It lay in ruins. I grabbed the phone and called Poo-Pah. He too had just heard the news and was on his way out the door to come home. I stared at the TV in disbelief, wondering what to do. I felt horror and fear. My heart was pounding hard.

The phone began ringing and ringing as the news quickly spread. Poo-Pah walked in the door, and I went to pieces. We quickly made arrangements for a friend to come stay with you. I had to go find my daughter, your mom.

I had worked as a nurse for ten years, and I heard that they had a triage unit at the YMCA, across from the Federal Building. I hoped my nursing experience might allow me access to those being found and treated. Poo-Pah and I jumped into the car and headed downtown. As we got onto the Broadway Extension, traffic was bumper to bumper, cars racing on the side of the road with their hazard lights flashing. The sounds of sirens filled the air. We exited onto Tenth Street and, unable to go any farther, walked the rest of the way to Fifth and Robinson, where the explosion had occurred. Glass was everywhere. People were everywhere. Confusion was everywhere.

We reached the blast area, but everything had been taped off by the police. Then people began running. They told us we had to leave the area because of the possibility there was another bomb. The police suggested we call the Red Cross. But the phone lines were tied up, and we couldn't reach anyone. So we decided to go to St. Anthony Hospital, where many of the victims were being treated. Then the waiting began, and we became trapped in what seemed like an unending nightmare.

They had us wait in what appeared to be a gymnasium. They put lists of victims' names and the hospitals where they were being treated on the walls. We searched every list for your mom's name, and called all the hospitals trying to find her. The wait was agonizing, and it went on for four long days and nights. We were helpless. All we could do was pray that your mom would be found alive.

On the fourth day, we were contacted and asked for medical X rays and dental records for identification purposes. Though we hoped for a miracle, we began to prepare for the worst. On the fifth day, Sunday, while our city was preparing for President Clinton and the Reverend Billy Graham to appear at a prayer service, we were waiting for notification of your mother's death. Then the waiting was over. Our worst fears became reality, and grief took hold. I could not pray. But many were praying for us. I listened for God's direction as we made arrangements for your mother's memorial service.

We are spiritual people. But through my life's journey I have seen God's work mostly outside the confines of church walls. We decided to have a celebration of your mother's life at a United Methodist church, where you attended Children's Day Out. There were songs and poems. Your Poo-Pah shared the importance of never forgetting to say "I love you" at every opportunity. I also had the speaker share what your mom might have said if she could have been there.

The outpouring of love in our city and across the nation was unparalleled. I can remember only one other time the country has come together in this way, after President Kennedy was assassinated. We received cards, letters, and contributions to your educational trust fund from friends and from people we did not even know. Rescuers risked their lives, hoping to find even one survivor. The loss of 168 lives, every victim someone's child, has put a mark upon this nation like no other. Everyone wanted to believe it was a terrorist act by someone from a foreign country. But it was one of our own.

My concern is great. The violence is terrifying. But I also know that love begets love, and hate begets hate. There are gangs here. There are drugs here. These things create a downward spiral into despair which evil feeds upon. But there is also good here. There is love here. So you must plant your own garden and decorate your own soul.

As I watch you grow, as I did your mother, I know that life is a journey and I pray it will be a safe one. I encourage you to think about your choices as you travel this road we call life.

I truly feel in my heart that your mom is a precious angel, watching over children as she did you. She has received a higher place with greater things to do. But her love will always be with you. Love does not die, people do.

I hope you, like your mom, will come to believe what I wrote in her Bible so many years ago: Happiness is by no means life's greatest goal, and it is not necessary to be happy all the time. But the habit of being pleased has sustained many a broken heart, just as a fretful inability to enjoy has dissolved many lives in bitterness.

I want you to know that those of us left here to love and guide you have big shoes to fill. But I will make sure you remember your mother, and what she stood for. Someone once said, "It's not duration of life, but donation." Your mother's donation was a legacy of love, generosity, integrity, honesty, courage, faith, and joy. We will forever hold her in our hearts as she surely holds our hearts in her angelic hands. In loving memory of your mother, Frankie Ann Merrell, born October 25, 1971, who became one of God's glorious angels on April 19, 1995. May God bless and keep you.

With much love,
Nana and Poo-Pah

"Don't forget justice—it is the test of
all we know as faith."
FATHER RICHARD MCBRIEN

Richard McBrien with nieces Elisabeth and Mary Catherine

Like most boys, Richard McBrien dreamed of being a baseball star. But his real vocation was the priesthood, and he followed in the footsteps of his uncle, already wearing the collar. Vatican Council II, McBrien says, changed his life, freeing him to be "the kind of theologian, priest, and Catholic that I am."

A professor at Notre Dame, general editor of The HarperCollins Encyclopedia of Catholicism, *and a regular contributor to the* National Catholic Reporter, *McBrien is known for his outspoken, sometimes controversial views on church reform. One of the most important things for kids to learn, he says, is that "life is relatively short, and like a vacation, it ends." McBrien's nieces, Mary Catherine, ten, and Elisabeth Grace, seven, live in West Hartford, Connecticut.*

Dear Mary Catherine and Elisabeth:

This letter doesn't come with colorful pictures or pop-ups, like most of your books, but I don't think that will matter very much. I only hope that the things I'm about to write won't appear too silly and old-fashioned, or just plain wrong by the time you're old enough to read and understand this.

After all, things change so fast in the world you're growing into. Your father and I didn't have our first television set until I was a sophomore in high school, and I was already teaching at Notre Dame before I had my first VCR. Elisabeth, you knew how to shut off the VCR before you could even talk.

I have a friend, Phil King, whom you've probably never met. He was one of my teachers in the seminary in Boston and is now teaching at Boston College. Phil is a Scripture scholar who specializes in a field known as biblical archaeology. Well, Phil may be a scholar's scholar, but he also has a lot of common-sense wisdom. One of his favorite sayings is that the older you get—he's seventy as I write this—the clearer it becomes what's really important in life: your faith, your health and your friends. I've always assumed that family was to be included with friends.

This letter is about the first of these: faith. According to our Catholic tradition, there are many different aspects to faith. Faith is belief (that's the most obvious). It is also commitment (which is really nothing more than doing what you say you believe in). And it is also a form of hope.

Through faith, we believe in things we do not see but are convinced are real nonetheless. You don't have to have faith that your Jack Russell terrier, Clancy, exists, because you see him every day and feel him jumping all over you in the morning when he bounds upstairs to wake you both up. But there are many things about life that people can't understand or figure out. Why do we get sick? Why is there so much suffering in the world? Why do little children get killed in accidents or in faraway places like Bosnia? Faith doesn't make all this evil go away, but it helps us to see how it might at least have some meaning. People who have faith often say, "We can't understand this now, but it must fit somehow into God's plan for us."

I've been a priest for over thirty-three years, but please don't think I have no difficulty with my own faith or with the faith of others. In fact, I often find myself turned off by people of faith. They seem too certain about everything, as if God were in constant touch with them, telling them what to think and what to do. But life isn't that simple, and no one is on a direct line with God, not even the Pope. We all have to muddle through somehow, fashioning our lives on our best estimates of what's right and wrong, true and false. The older I get, the more I realize that life isn't an exact science.

For me, the most important aspect of faith is not belief, but commitment—practicing what we say we believe. By faith, we commit ourselves to a particular kind of life. Instead of measuring everything by how much money we make or how much property we own or how much power and prestige we gain, we measure our lives by how much good we do with the talents and resources we've been given.

Mary Catherine, you may still remember your Grandmother McBrien, even though you were only four and a half when she died. She was my mother, and I loved her just like you love your mother now. I will always remember what she said to us so many times: The way to find happiness and fulfillment in life is by "doing for others." And that's how she lived her life.

Every day, she worked her regular eight-hour shift as a nurse at one Hartford hospital, and then she went to a different hospital and worked another eight-hour, private-duty shift through the rest of the night. But she didn't do this to make extra money for herself. She did it because she wanted to provide for her family. Not only to feed and to clothe us, but to see that we got a good education and had an opportunity to make something of ourselves. That's what faith-as-commitment means. Not just believing in something, but doing something—for others.

The Jesuits have a wonderful way of putting it: They view their mission in the world as a "faith that does justice." For me, that's the essence of Catholicism. It's not about the Pope or about bishops or about this moral issue or that. True religious faith is a faith that does justice. The New Testament tells us that a faith without works is dead. And St. John said that whoever claims that they love God but hate their neighbor is a liar. Those are strong words, but they go to the heart of the matter.

Unfortunately, American society today is moving sharply away from this ethic. There is far too much scapegoating of others—the poor, people of color, gays and lesbians, immigrants—as an explanation for the decline in our middle-class standard of living. "I'm up, pull up the ladder," seems to have replaced "Do unto others as you would have them do unto you."

Sometimes I wonder what our church will look like 100 years from now. I feel confident that it won't look much like it does today. In fact, I expect that it will be very different even in your own lifetimes, when you're as old as I am now. Women will be recognized by then as equal partners in the church. There will be women priests and women bishops and someday a woman Pope.

Mary Catherine, you're already doing something that, just a few years ago, would have been unthinkable: You're serving at Mass. I shall always treasure the wonderful feeling of having you serve, for the first time, at a Mass I presided over at St. Helena's. Your grandmother would have been very proud of you. I can still picture her sitting in her regular pew in the front of the church, off to my left. And, Elisabeth, I expect you'll take your turn soon, too. Grandmother used to say that she agreed with all of my views on the church except women priests. But in her final years, I suspect she no longer disagreed even on that. Your grandmother was a feminist before the word was invented.

In the end, there is a fine line between faith and hope. The New Testament speaks of faith as the "assurance of things hoped for." To believe in something or in someone is really to hope in something or in someone. And to be committed is also a form of hope—a hope that your commitment to a particular set of values or to a particular person is truly worthwhile, that by choosing this path in life rather than that you will find true happiness and fulfillment forever.

I hope that faith will have that kind of positive, nurturing presence in your lives, and in the lives of your own children. You'll find, however, that it is not something you can turn on and off like a faucet. The older you become, the more you realize how fragile such faith is, and how elusive. But you make the most of what you have. And, believe me, love will supply the rest. The love of your parents, your sister, your Grandmother "Mimi," your aunts and uncles, your cousins, and someday your husband and your own children. But, in the midst of everything, don't forget justice. It is the test of all that we know as faith.

Love,
Uncle Richard

Ever since she was three years old, Holly Scholles wanted to be a healer. She considered medical school, but decided to become a midwife instead. Eighteen years and four hundred babies later, Scholles is acutely conscious that each woman's path through pregnancy, labor, and delivery is a unique journey of empowerment, separation, and surrender. Her own children, Genevieve, seventeen, and Evan, four, were both born at home.

Fascination with childbirth led Scholles eventually to study birth practices in different cultures. In Portland, Oregon, she divides her time between midwifery, work on a doctoral degree in anthropology, and her efforts to provide her children with essential life skills.

To My Dearest Children:

It is well past midnight. The telephone's ring jolts me awake. "Please come over right now," the voice says. "She needs you!" I dress quickly, kiss your sleeping faces, load my equipment, and set out into a cold, clear night.

Driving along the empty streets, I pray for blessings on my head, my heart, and my hands, so that I may serve skillfully and with compassion. As the car heater works to blast away the cold, I think of you cuddled in your warm beds: Will it be three or thirty hours before I see you again? What will this night hold for me? Will I bear witness to an easy labor and birth, or to a difficult struggle for new life to emerge?

Midwife means "with woman." After twenty years of midwifing, of being with women as they change and grow along with their bellies, I have learned that the patterns of birth are the patterns of life.

Like all life, birth cannot be controlled or managed, although we often convince ourselves that it can. Life reveals itself moment by moment, the uncertainty often held at bay by our expectations. Beware of expectations: While they make us feel secure and certain, they also burden us, blinding us to life's unfolding.

I see this often with laboring women. After reading and talking to friends, women end their pregnancies confident that labor will be "manageable," with clear time frames and predictable sensations. The truth is

"Like all life, birth cannot really be controlled."
HOLLY SCHOLLES

Holly Scholles with children Genevieve and Evan

that each labor is unique, just as each infant born is unique. The general pattern is recognizable, but the individual variations are endless.

Time and again, I have seen a woman coast through early labor, intently "breathing through" contractions. "The pain is manageable," she says, "I can handle this." As hours pass, her baby no closer to birth, physical and emotional exhaustion force her to let go, to allow her labor to be wild and unmanageable, intense and earth-shattering. As she surrenders to the process, drawing on inner strengths never tapped before, I stay with her, supporting and encouraging, but unable to do her work. Every woman gives birth completely alone, no matter how many coaches and assistants she may have with her. She must find her power, draw on ancient cell memory, and bring forth new life.

As the baby passes down the birth canal, women often moan "I can't; I'm afraid. I'm splitting in two." And I respond, "You can, you are. It is scary. You are splitting into two—you and your baby. You can do it." And she does: Opens up, lets go, moves through her fear, releases her newborn. Brings forth joy and love, a new family, new life.

As you grow into adults, well-meaning people may encourage you to develop your strengths and eliminate your weaknesses. But I encourage you to understand and to embrace your human frailties, those dark parts of yourself that you may prefer not to see. Every "good" quality has its "bad" counterpart, and you must understand both to have a full and balanced life. You are simultaneously generous and stingy, honest and secretive, lazy and hardworking, caring and cold, courageous and fearful—to various degrees at different times. For example, people often think of anger as "bad" and to be avoided. But anger is an appropriate response to injustice. Anger also can be a signal, a clue that you need to look deeper, that perhaps you are hiding something from yourself, making excuses. I see this with laboring women.

A woman having her third baby. Her other children birthed quickly, easily, but this one is slow-going. The woman walks and breathes and relaxes and changes positions and breathes some more, and labor slowly moves ahead. The woman begins telling herself: It's too hard, it's unfair, my babies are supposed to come fast. She feels sorry for herself, trapped in her expectations. "I just can't do this," she says in a small, sad voice. I look her straight in the eye and say, "Yes, you can." "No, I can't," she says, less sad now, more irritated. "I know that you can birth this baby just fine," I say. "No, I can't," she says again, angry now, sure that I don't understand how difficult this really is, how hard she's working. But as her anger rises, she stops trying and simply does it, her mind uniting with her body in a flash of hormones that moves the labor along. Later, baby in arms, she says, "I was so mad at you, but I guess that helped me to let go." And so it does.

Whenever you feel ashamed of some part of yourself, don't shove it back or ignore it. Bring it forward, look at it, see how it serves you—what fear it might ease or hide, what boundary it protects. Feel it, embrace it, because you can't make anger, or fear, or any other "negative" part of you go away by shoving it down. It will grow from your neglect, and manifest itself eventually.

A woman having her second baby. Her first child died shortly after birth from severe defects. She had worked as a hospital X-ray technician and blamed herself for her child's death. Her due date comes and goes, but she has no contractions. Day after day passes without sign of labor. All is fine physically. So one afternoon, we talk. "Why do you think your baby isn't born yet?" I ask. She says, "Well, at least now, inside me, she's safe. Once she's born, I can't protect her anymore." And so the truth slowly comes out: old grief, fear, guilt, all mixed together. As we talk, she allows herself to recognize, to own those dark places inside herself. Their power slowly ebbs. Her body softens and opens. The next morning, as the sun rises, she pushes out a healthy, beautiful daughter.

Birth and life reveal many such powerful moments. As you grow and choose your life's path, be open to mystery, to what is real but not easily understood. I have seen many miracles, large and small, some with happy outcomes, others with sad, yet still miraculous, endings.

A woman having her first child. Throughout the pregnancy, she is plagued by fear that something is wrong. Her labor starts strong and continues unabated. At delivery, serious complications with the placenta cut off oxygen to her son. He is born warm but still, without pulse or breath. Emergency resuscitation starts his heart beating, but his brain does not similarly skip into aliveness. He lies in a small bed, breathing on his own, only a few thin tubes marring his perfect beauty. The doctors tell her: "His body is strong. But he will never leave his bed, will never play, talk, or think." As she prepares to leave the hospital for the night, she lifts her son into her arms, cradling him. She tells him that she loves him; that she is so glad he came into her life for this little time, and that he will always be her little boy. But now, she says, you don't need to stay any longer. You can go back home to heaven now. And she gently lays him in his bassinet. As she walks across the hospital parking lot toward her car, her strong-hearted son, suddenly, unexpectedly, peacefully, dies.

The opposite of death is birth, not life. Just as life begins with birth, life is completed by death.

Now it is three o'clock in the morning, one day later than when I started this letter, and I have just returned home. Tomorrow is Special Treat Day at school, and weeks ago I signed up for cookies. I am standing in the kitchen, bone-tired, waiting for the last batch of oatmeal chocolate chips to bake. I think I'll write my advice in a nice, concise list, so that you can skip straight to the end if you'd like.

Walk your own path. Don't let fear and expectations, your own or those of others, control you.

Embrace all parts of yourself, limitations as well as strengths, and don't be afraid to look with clear eyes at the "dark" parts of your soul.

Be humble in the face of mystery, recognizing that while you are part of the web of life, you are only a part. Accept that you are not all-powerful, that "control" is neither possible nor desirable. Surrender, and trust that life finds its own best expression. As I am always saying, "Things will work out as they're supposed to."

Be compassionate and live joyfully.

I am eternally grateful that I am your mother; I have learned much from you.

> I will love each of you always and forever.
> Your Mom

Acknowledgments

This book could not have come into being without the efforts of many people. We are grateful to:

Jeannye Thornton, associate editor at *U.S. News & World Report*, for pouring her heart, her spirit, and her soul into this book. Her ideas greatly enriched the list of contributors—Jeannye seemed to know exactly who was right for this book and where to find them. And once the list of letter writers was assembled, she spent hours on the phone with them, sharing their stories, their hopes for the future, their worries and fears for their children. We could not have carried out this project without her.

Jim Lo Scalzo, *U.S. News* staff photographer, for giving up any summer plans he may have had to drive in large loops around the country taking elegant portraits of the contributors.

Merrill McLoughlin and Michael Ruby, then co-editors of *U.S. News*, for giving us the time and space to produce this book on a tight deadline, extending their encouragement and goodwill at every opportunity, and offering an enthusiastic audience as the project emerged.

Kathy Bushkin, director of editorial administration at *U.S. News*, for her belief in the book, which helped it become reality, and for her deft judgment and managerial wizardry, which smoothed the way for everyone involved.

Mark Godfrey, then *U.S. News* photography director, for bringing to the book his extensive photographic expertise and keen editorial eye.

Lee Rainie, *U.S. News* managing editor, for helping shape the idea for the book, and offering his insight, intuition, and editing wisdom on a regular basis during its production.

Caroline Little, *U.S. News* deputy general counsel, for guiding us faithfully through the work on the book and treating it as a labor of love, and George Washington University law professor C. Thomas Dienes, for his invaluable assistance.

U.S. News associate editors Linda Creighton and Joannie Schrof, administrative assistant Anna Dickens, chief of fact-checking Kathleen Phillips, editorial assistant Nick Merlino, and interviews administrator Ron Wilson, for devoting considerable effort to this project, and helping in many ways, large and small.

Ric Cox, executive director of the America's Awards, for providing us with lists and biographies of award winners, two of whom are included in this book.

And Jonathan Karp, our editor at Random House, who was always there, always patient, always smart, and nearly always right.

Most of all, we are grateful to the contributors, among them those who invested time and enthusiasm in the project but whose letters, for reasons of space, geography, or mix, we were unable to include. We thank them.

ABOUT THE EDITOR

ERICA GOODE is an assistant managing editor at *U.S. News & World Report*, where she has worked since 1987. She has received numerous awards for her writing on mental health and other social issues. A native of Ann Arbor, Michigan, Goode received her bachelor's degree from the University of Michigan and her master's degree in social psychology from the University of California at Santa Cruz. She has also been a staff writer at the *San Francisco Chronicle* and has written for *Vogue, Mirabella,* and *Psychology Today.*

ABOUT THE TYPE

This book was set in Weiss, a typeface designed by a German artist, Emil Rudolf Weiss (1875–1942). The designs of the roman and italic were completed in 1928 and 1931 respectively. The Weiss types are rich, well-balanced, and even in color, and they reflect the subtle skill of a fine calligrapher.